The New York Times

PUBLIC PROFILES

Transgender Activists and Celebrities

THE NEW YORK TIMES EDITORIAL STAFF

Published in 2019 by New York Times Educational Publishing
in association with The Rosen Publishing Group, Inc.
29 East 21st Street, New York, NY 10010

First Edition

The New York Times
Alex Ward: Editorial Director, Book Development
Brenda Hutchings: Senior Photo Editor/Art Buyer
Phyllis Collazo: Photo Rights/Permissions Editor
Heidi Giovine: Administrative Manager

Rosen Publishing
Jacob R. Steinberg: Director of Content Development
Greg Tucker: Creative Director
Brian Garvey: Art Director
Julia Bosson: Editor

Cataloging-in-Publication Data
Names: New York Times Company.
Title: Transgender activists and celebrities / edited by the New York Times editorial staff.
Description: New York : The New York Times Educational Publishing, 2019. | Series: Public profiles | Includes glossary and index.
Identifiers: ISBN 9781642820287 (pbk.) | ISBN 9781642820270 (library bound) | ISBN 9781642820263 (ebook)
Subjects: LCSH: Transgender people—Juvenile literature. | Gender identity—Juvenile literature.
Classification: LCC HQ77.9 T736 2019 | DDC 306.76'8—dc23

Manufactured in the United States of America

On the cover: traffic_analyzer/Getty Images.

Contents

CHAPTER 3

Television

CHAPTER 4

Pop Culture

CHAPTER 5

Writers and Activists

Introduction

IN 2013, Netflix's "Orange is the New Black" broke ground when it featured the story of a transgender inmate, played by the actress and activist Laverne Cox. The following year, Cox was featured on the cover of Time magazine with the headline "The Transgender Tipping Point." Indeed, it did seem as though transgender stories had finally found their way into the spotlight: that same year, Jill Soloway's "Transparent" premiered on Amazon, featuring the aftermath of a father's late-in-life transition on his family. In 2015, Caitlyn Jenner announced her transition on the cover of Vanity Fair and starred in her own reality show that debuted on E!. Meanwhile, a teenager named Gavin Grimm sued his school for preventing him from using the boy's bathroom, and President Obama issued a directive ordering the military to allow transgender troops to serve openly. "The Danish Girl" and "3 Generations" swept the box office, and several years later, Chile's "A Fantastic Woman" won an Oscar for Best Foreign Language Film.

In other words, the 2010s have resulted in a sea change in the transgender rights movement. For the first time in history, transgender issues have entered the mainstream, and transgender men and women have become household names. Through sports, film, television, arts, and politics, transgender individuals have made their presence and their struggle for equality felt, supported in part by the reporting of publications like The New York Times.

Along with the increased prominence of transgender stories has come a series of debates: Is visibility enough? Does it matter if a script is written by a transgender person, or if a transgender individual is played by a cis-gendered (someone who identifies with his or her gender assigned at birth) actor? Who has the right to tell transgender stories?

Laverne Cox broke barriers as a transgender star of the Netflix show "Orange Is the New Black."

The articles in this book feature the stories of transgender men and women whose lives have guided and informed our understanding of transgender issues. Some of these figures are complicated, such as Caitlyn Jenner, whose transition was celebrated as a boon to transgender visibility, but whose support of conservative politicians has resulted in a significant amount of backlash. There is also Chelsea Manning, the army soldier who was prosecuted for releasing classified documents to WikiLeaks and whose transition in prison was widely followed. There are the writers, filmmakers, and artists whose work has been highlighting transgender stories in the mainstream, from Daniela Vega, the star of the Oscar-winning film "A Fantastic Woman," to Zackary Drucker and Rhys Ernst, two producers on the television show "Transparent." There are also those whose names may not be as recognizable, such as Sylvia Rivera and Julia Serano, but whose contributions to the fight for transgender equality have been felt widely.

Every story in this book is the story of a pioneer. These individuals have faced and overcome barriers in their respective industries and have paved a path for the lives and works of the next generation, and in the process, they have shaped our discussion of transgender issues, stories, and rights. And as much as their accomplishments deserve to be recognized, their stories also point to the work that is still to come.

CHAPTER I

Models and Athletes

The worlds of sports and fashion may not appear to have much in common, but both have been at the forefront of transgender visibility issues. Because the industries typically separate participants by gender, the addition of transgender participants has forced fashion and sports to rethink categorization and binaries. This chapter features the stories of athletes and models as they challenge cultural expectations of what bodies are capable of.

Transgender Man Is on Women's Team

BY KATIE THOMAS | NOV. 1, 2010

MONDAY WAS A lazy day for Kye Allums, a typically busy junior playing Division I basketball at George Washington University. Without any classes or practice on his schedule, Allums woke up late, stopped in at a team meeting, worked on a class project, then took an afternoon nap.

But Monday was anything but ordinary because it was the day the world would learn about the decision Allums had embarked on one year earlier: to come out as a transgender man playing on a women's basketball team.

Advocates for transgender athletes said they believed Allums was the first Division I college basketball player to compete publicly as a transgender person, although not the first to play as a college athlete. In a statement, a George Washington official said Allums would remain on the women's basketball team.

Earlier this year, the university changed the roster published on its Web site to reflect Allums's name change, from Kay-Kay to Kye, and future references will use male pronouns.

He noted that he was biologically identical to any other female, but said, "I just would prefer for people to call me a he."

"I decided to do it because I was uncomfortable not being able to be myself," Allums, 21, said in a telephone interview Monday, hours after an article about his experience was published on the Web site Outsports.com. "Just having to hear the words 'she' and 'her,' it was really starting to bother me."

Helen Carroll, the sports project director at the National Center for Lesbian Rights, said she expected other Division I athletes to follow in Allums's footsteps. Already, she said, "we see younger and younger children, middle school and high school kids that are in athletics and are playing who are transgender."

Carroll is the co-author of a report released last month meant to serve as a guide for schools and universities to develop fair policies for transgender athletes.

Allums, a guard who started 20 of the Colonials' 28 games last season, said he grew up feeling that he was a man, and although he identified as a lesbian in high school, he came to the conclusion that he was transgender while he was a freshman in college.

In addition to the expected stress of breaking the news to family and friends, Allums said being a member of the women's team complicated matters. He worried that he might lose his George Washington scholarship.

"Being an athlete intensifies everything," he said. "I'm seen more. I'm in newspapers. I travel. I represent the school more so than a normal student would because they're under wraps."

The first people Allums told were his teammates, who, after initial disbelief, offered their support, he said. After that, he said he often relied on the team to break the news to others.

"They started to say things for me, like, 'No, don't call Kye her, say him,' " said Allums, who is an interior design major and plans to pursue a career as an architect or personal trainer. "They would say it to everybody."

Allums told his coach, Mike Bozeman, in June. Bozeman said in a statement that the "George Washington University women's basketball program, including myself, support Kye's right to make this decision."

Erik Christianson, a spokesman for the N.C.A.A., said in an e-mail that the association was planning a review of its policies toward transgender athletes but currently recommended following the gender classification on a student's identification documents, like a driver's license. George Washington officials have said that the N.C.A.A. told them that Allums was eligible for the women's team because he had not undergone hormone treatments.

Allums said he would like to receive the treatments but had held off because he did not want to jeopardize his spot on the team.

He is looking forward to Nov. 13, when Allums and the team will compete at the Best Buy Classic in Minneapolis. The game will be his public debut as a transgender man playing on a women's team, but it will take place on friendly turf. Allums grew up in St. Paul and the nearby town of Hugo, and the stands will be packed with old friends. "We're ready to go," Allums said of the team, adding that the transition had improved his game. "I'm able to just focus on basketball now. My outside life is not really a distraction to me."

For Transgender Triathlete, a Top Finish in New York Is Secondary

BY FREDERICK DREIER | AUG. 5, 2011

AFTER FINISHING in Central Park on Sunday, participants in the New York City Triathlon will huddle around the results pages, analyzing split times and category rankings.

Chris Mosier, 31, will not be among them.

Mosier is transgendered and will be competing in the triathlon for the first time as a man. In 2009, he completed the 1.1-mile swim, 25-mile bike and 6.1-mile run in 2 hours 39 minutes, good enough for 27th place in the women's 25-29 category. Now racing in the men's 30-34 field, one of the most competitive in the race, Mosier says he will be lucky to finish in the middle of the pack. Instead of focusing on results, Mosier said, he just wants to enjoy racing his peers.

"Until recently I still was holding on to that idea of finishing in a very high place in my category," Mosier said. "Now I don't expect to finish as high. I just want to enjoy being comfortable in the race."

The tradeoff is small for Mosier, who says he has struggled with his gender identity since he was 4 years old. Mosier said he was picked on in high school and college for adopting an androgynous appearance. In 2010, after years of contemplation, he legally changed his documentation to male and started receiving testosterone injections.

Triathlon follows International Olympic Committee rules, which require transgender athletes to wait two years after having surgery and hormone treatment before they can compete. A USA Triathlon representative said the rules also apply to amateur athletes.

But John Korff, owner of the New York City Triathlon, said he would not bar Mosier from competing.

"This is an age grouper who is out to have fun, God bless him," Korff said. "And I don't think anybody is getting an inherent advantage going from a woman to a man."

The question of performance gains because of gender change has hindered transgender female athletes for decades. The United States Tennis Association barred the transgender tennis player Renée Richards from playing as a woman in the 1976 United States Open. The golfer Lana Lawless, who had gender reassignment surgery in 2005, sued the L.P.G.A. in 2010, claiming that the league's "female at birth" rule violated California civil rights law. Michelle Dumaresq, a former Canadian downhill mountain biking champion, eventually left her sport after other Canadian racers protested her involvement.

Transgender male athletes like Mosier have not experienced the same legal hurdles. In 2010, the N.C.A.A. cleared Kye Allums, who identifies as male but was born female, to play for the George Washington University women's basketball team, provided Allums did not undergo testosterone treatment.

That does not mean female-to-male athletes have an easy life in sports. Helen Carroll, sports project director for the National Center for Lesbian Rights, said transgender males often face harsher social pushback than transgender females.

"Oddly enough, the worst behavior in terms of teasing, taunting and threats is against female-to-male athletes," Carroll said. "There is the belief that even with testosterone, a woman can't be as competitive as a man."

Mosier says he still experiences intimidation because of his gender on a regular basis, and he declined to name his place of employment or his hometown for fear of reprisal. But the tension he faces as a transgender athlete, Mosier said, is less than it was when he was a female athlete who identified as male.

"It is difficult to see old photos of myself, or to think about past memories, because there were some really unhappy moments during those times," Mosier said.

Mosier said he felt awkward standing on the start line alongside women, and spectators taunted him for his androgynous appearance. He felt out of place in a women's bathing suit during swim sessions at the John Jay College pool. In the locker room women scowled at him, or simply asked him to leave. During the Fifth Avenue Mile road race in 2009, a police officer asked him if he was in the wrong gender category.

The experiences did little to sour Mosier's love for endurance sports. A lifelong athlete, Mosier began competing in New York Road Runner's events after moving to New York City in 2005. He completed his first triathlon in 2009, winning the "first-timer" division at the Flat as a Pancake race in Staten Island. Mosier said he delayed his gender transition because of his passion for endurance sports.

"I was really starting to do well, and I thought if I gave myself one more year, what kind of results could I get?" Mosier said. "I decided it is more important for me to feel comfortable in my life when I am not competing than for me to finish on the podium of a race."

Loren Cannon, a transgender triathlete from Eureka, Calif., said he also had to refocus his goals after his transition from female to male. Cannon, a professor of philosophy at Humboldt State University, formerly competed as an elite female triathlete, and said that he now values top results more than he did as an elite woman. Cannon finished third out of 20 competitors at the 2009 Try for Fun triathlon in Sacramento.

"I got a lot of awards as a woman, and it really felt good to win an award as a man," Cannon said.

Mosier, who has yet to win as a man, has an ambitious racing calendar ahead. On Sept. 18, he will race the Adirondack 540, a 540-mile bicycle race that is a qualifying event for the Race Across America, a solo race from California to New Jersey. On Oct. 2, he will race the Ironman 70.3 triathlon in Pennsylvania.

He also hopes to advance transgender issues and show transgender people that endurance sports can help develop an identity for those who have grown up without one.

"Most people assume that men are naturally better athletes and write off the ability of a trans guy switching over to compete as male because he isn't seen as competition," Mosier said. "Regardless of gender, I will beat a lot of athletes at races, and I will get beat by some."

Just Being Himself, in a Professional Women's Hockey League

BY MATT HIGGINS | OCT. 19, 2016

BUFFALO — He changed his voice mail recording and created a new email address. He updated his LinkedIn profile, too, to reflect his new name.

With those details settled, and the National Women's Hockey League season about to begin, Harrison Browne, who was born Hailey Browne and identifies as a man, was ready to debut as the first openly transgender athlete in professional team sports in North America.

Browne, a 23-year-old wing for the Buffalo Beauts, first heard his new name over the public-address system here at HarborCenter during player introductions for the season opener, on Oct. 7 against the Boston Pride. He heard it again when he scored his team's lone goal in a 4-1 loss.

"If somebody asked me later down the road what my favorite moment was, that will definitely be one of the top," Browne said about the goal call, an audio clip of which he has saved. "I would have loved for it to have been a game-winning goal. It was amazing just to hear the crowd cheer so loud. I was elated. The timing was perfect."

Bruce Jenner, a former Olympic decathlon champion, came out as a transgender woman in 2015 and took the name Caitlyn Jenner. And Chris Mosier, a professional triathlete who was born a woman, publicly identified himself as a transgender man in 2010 and competed for the United States national team at the sprint duathlon world championships in June. There have been transgender athletes on college teams, too.

But no active player in a professional team sport in North America is believed to have come out publicly as transgender before Browne did so in an interview with ESPN published hours before the season opener.

The Buffalo Beauts' Harrison Browne, who played last season as Hailey Browne, scored in his team's season opener in the National Women's Hockey League.

"When Harrison came to me and wanted it to be public, and wanted us to respect his name and his pronoun and for him to play as his authentic self, the first thought was, how can I support this player, and what are the next steps to do so?" said Dani Rylan, commissioner of the four-team N.W.H.L., which is now in its second season of operation.

The N.W.H.L. has changed Browne's name and pronouns on his player profile on the league website. And the league is working with You Can Play — an organization that works to ensure athletes are not discriminated against because of sexual orientation or gender identity — to create a policy on transgender players that respects the rights of athletes and concerns about fair play.

"It's important for us to get it right, and we're confident we'll get it right," said Rylan, who expects a policy to be in place this season.

Browne said he was not motivated to come out by thoughts of being a pioneer.

"When I came out, it wasn't 'I want to do this to be an advocate,' " he said at a Starbucks on a sunny autumn morning last week. "I want to do this because I want to feel comfortable in my own playing environment, my workplace, because it's my job. That's why I did it. I've seen all these posts where people say I'm an inspiration, and people thanking me for what I'm doing, just being myself."

Browne had come out to his family, friends and teammates by his sophomore year at the University of Maine, where he played women's hockey. But he continued to be known publicly as Hailey Browne, including during the 2015-16 N.W.H.L. season, in which he had five goals and seven assists in 18 games for the Beauts.

"Supporting a teammate goes beyond the rink," said Ric Seiling, the Beauts' general manager and coach, who played 10 N.H.L. seasons. "Harrison has been a great team player for the team. We need to support Harrison in his decision."

Browne's nickname in high school was Harry, he said, and it stuck with him.

"It was comforting to me to not be called a female name," he said. "I gravitated toward it, and that's what it took."

For now, Browne's change is in name only. He has said he will delay a physical transition, including hormone treatments, until after his hockey career is over.

Until then, Browne, who is a wiry 5 feet 4, has to deal with occasional slip-ups.

"Some people call me 'sir'; some call me 'ma'am,' " he said. "I don't get upset about that. How would they know? You just have to keep in mind that one day it won't be like that."

At practice last week for the Beauts, who are 1-2 heading into a home game Sunday against the Connecticut Whale, teammates described Browne as a speedy, gritty wing who plays an in-your-face game. A humble workout warrior who led the team with 20 pull-ups during fitness testing, he spends long hours crocheting on team bus rides and is boisterous in the locker room.

At home, he adores his pet ferrets, said defender Paige Harrington and forward Devon Skeats, who share a house with Browne.

"He is such a strong person," said Harrington, who had never known a transgender person before. "He's comfortable with himself. He's hard-working. He's encouraging to others. He's the perfect person to be the first to come out and be transgender in women's hockey."

Skeats played in a professional women's league in Austria before the N.W.H.L. and had a transgender teammate who had begun a physical transition and was receiving hormone supplements.

"He was my best friend on the team there," she said. "So it was kind of cool when I came here and met Brownie."

Skeats added: "It's what he wants to do, what he wants to be, and I'm happy for him. There's nothing different. He's just another teammate."

In the long hockey tradition, Skeats and Harrington referred to Browne by a nickname: Brownie, the same one he had last season. Among the Beauts, there was seldom mention of "Harrison."

Seiling, the coach, said he called Browne Harrison only when he was angry.

"To all of us, Harrison is Brownie," Seiling said. "All athletes have some sort of nickname, or last name. When I start using a different name, they automatically know, I screwed up."

But out in the wider world, there is no negative connotation to the name Harrison — just a public and private life finally in alignment, and a sound he savors.

"I have people like you coming out, saying, 'Hey, Harrison,' " Browne said to a reporter who met him at the coffee shop. "It's nice to hear people call me by my name. It's definitely very freeing."

A Model's Life, Chapter 2: Will the Fashion World Accept Andreja Pejic As a Woman?

BY MATTHEW SCHNEIER | SEPT. 5, 2014

ANDREJA PEJIC, who stands 6-foot-1 in stocking feet, and a good deal taller than that in heels, looks every bit the model. She is possessed of bottle-blond hair that falls past her shoulders, full lips, a wasp waist and a pair of Cindy Crawford beauty marks just north of her upper lip. (Even Ms. Crawford has only one.)

On Labor Day, just back in New York from a vacation with her mother and grandmother in Italy, Ms. Pejic, 23, arrived at her agency's office in a leather pencil skirt from Ports 1961 and a silk Calvin Klein blouse, a picture of elegance compromised only by the occasional glimpse of a peach lace bra.

It was a far cry from the look she cultivated when she first appeared on the fashion scene typically dressed in a punkish, provocative mixture of men's and women's wear. "I had fun with androgyny, I had fun being rock 'n' roll," she said. "But now it's time to be chic."

Outside, hundreds of young models, most not as striking or as experienced as Ms. Pejic, are wandering wide-eyed through a city many of them barely know, portfolios in hand. They are going from casting call to casting call, rarely knowing their shifting schedules more than a few hours in advance, in the hope of being selected for runway shows. They have descended en masse upon New York for fashion week, which began on Thursday and runs through next week. Later, they will arrive, as if by airlift, in London, then Milan, then Paris, as the international round of fashion weeks moves across the globe.

But Ms. Pejic is no longer pounding the pavement. She is taking meetings, exploring collaborations and hoping to secure a spot in a top show. The signal difference between her and every other wraith-thin

The model Andreja Pejic, in Madison Square Park. She is in New York for fashion week.

young woman swarming the environs of Madison Square Park, where a concentration of top modeling agencies have offices, is that she has already had a yearslong and very successful career as a male model named Andrej Pejic.

And now, after several months away from the business, she is waiting to see whether a major designer — indeed, the entire fashion establishment — will accept her as a woman.

Four years ago, Ms. Pejic arrived in Europe and became a fast favorite of editors and designers, especially those with a rebellious bent. Her first professional job landed her on the cover of Oyster, an Australian fashion magazine, and during her first Paris season, she was cast by men's wear designers including Paul Smith, John Galliano, Raf Simons and Jean Paul Gaultier, who became a major supporter. "I worked a suit very well," Ms. Pejic said.

Androgyny had always been a major part of her (back then, his) appeal. She had alternated in her youth between embracing her femininity and concealing it, first as a child growing up in a refugee camp in Serbia during the Bosnian War, then as an preadolescent émigré to Australia. The Australian agency that signed her as a male model, after a scout found her working behind the counter of a Melbourne McDonald's on New Year's Eve 2007, loved her resemblance to its top female model, Jessica Hart. Australian Vogue later photographed them side by side.

But what Ms. Pejic did not disclose to her agents was that her androgyny was caused in part by Androcur, a synthetic hormone she was taking to suppress her development. She had already privately acknowledged her gender dysphoria and had begun treatment, first secretly, then with the support of her family. It was the thought of raising money for an eventual transition that spurred her to model at all.

Her androgyny endeared her to some, but in other corners of the male modeling world, pressure to conform grew.

"When I first went to Milan, my agent said you have to give off a strong, masculine energy," Ms. Pejic said. "They don't like campiness.

They like boys to appear straight and to appear masculine. I quickly learned the game of it, and how to navigate around it."

Even so, a nagging fear set in: that modeling, initially undertaken to make her transition possible, was taking her farther from it. "I would call my mum," she said, "and say, 'Who's ever going to accept me as a woman if the whole world knows me as a boy?' "

But in following seasons, Mr. Gaultier cast her not only in his men's wear show and print ad campaign, but also in his haute couture show, in the coveted show-closing position traditionally known as the mariée — the bride.

From then on, Ms. Pejic worked continuously, racking up magazine shoots in both men's and women's clothing. She was featured in ads for men's wear by Marc Jacobs, Neil Barrett and Martyn Bal, and for women's wear by Silvian Heach and the Dutch retailer Hema, for which she modeled a push-up bra.

Her popularity surged. According to Stephan Moskovic, the founder and editor of Models.com, which compiles unofficial rankings, by 2011, Ms. Pejic climbed to No. 11 of the site's list of top male models, and her profile on the site received the most Facebook "likes" of any model — male or female.

More and more, Ms. Pejic was pursued by magazines looking to shoot her in women's clothing, or a combination of men's and women's clothing. An eager press flocked to tell her story and explain, if it could, her otherworldly beauty. New York Magazine put her on the cover of its fall fashion issue in 2011, profiling her as "The Prettiest Boy in the World" with "only the faintest trace of an Adam's apple" and peach-fuzzed cheeks. No hormone treatments were mentioned.

The androgynous life might have been satisfying initially; Ms. Pejic was working regularly and well-known enough that playing "masculine" was not only no longer required, but barely sought. But it wasn't enough. Tired of putting off her dream any longer, she decided to undergo sex reassignment surgery.

"I wasn't sure going into this what would happen with my career," she said. "There are agents that would tell me: 'Don't ever do it. Don't transition. You'll lose everything.' "

But at the end of last year, she stepped back from the fashion world and found a surgeon to perform the operation. She prefers not to disclose specifics about the procedure other than to say, "I identify as a woman first but I am also proudly trans."

Ms. Pejic is not the first transgender model to achieve success. Transgender women have appeared on the runway and in fashion magazines (albeit in some cases without acknowledging being transgender publicly) since before the word was coined, including April Ashley in the 1960s, Tula in the 1970s, Teri Toye in the 1980s and Connie Fleming in the 1990s.

Transgender models are now becoming more common and more open. The Brazilian model Lea T, a muse to Riccardo Tisci of Givenchy, appeared in the label's ad campaigns and on its catwalk. In January, Barneys New York debuted an advertising campaign featuring transgender models, with great success. Some already had runway experience; others signed to agencies following the ads' debut.

"It was truly thrilling to see how receptive the media and public was to the campaign," Dennis Freedman, Barneys's creative director, wrote in an email.

Nor is Ms. Pejic the only transgender model hoping to work during this New York Fashion Week. May Simon, a transgender woman represented by Click Model Management, who was one of the models from the Barneys campaign, is in New York attending castings, her agent, Harold Mindel, confirmed, and appeared in the Chromat show on Thursday.

Stav Strashko, who appears androgynous but does not identify as transgender, is male and on the women's board at his agency, One Management, the first man to be so represented. He already has been booked for some New York shows, including DKNY on Sunday, said Scott Lipps, One's owner and president. "It's become more apparent that people are very open to this idea," Mr. Lipps said.

But Ms. Pejic is in the unique position of having transitioned in the public eye. "In the beginning, I was worried there are too many shots of me as a boy out there," she said. "Now I'm at a point where I know my past doesn't make me any less of a woman today. I can be proud of it. I don't have to bury it."

Instead, she has made her story a key component of her public persona. She has sold a memoir based on her experience to Penguin Books Australia, and hopes to find an American publisher. With a filmmaker friend, Eric Miclette, she is creating a documentary about her experience. They are soliciting support to finish the film via a Kickstarter campaign starting today.

It falls to her new agency, the Society Management, to facilitate what is essentially a rebranding. "I think that a lot of people would associate her with a niche market, something really cool or even underground," said Christopher Michael, an executive agent there. "I think that she represents so much more than that ... she herself is much more interested in a global audience."

Unlike her former agency, DNA Model Management, which has men's and women's boards, the Society Management represents only women.

"There were some people who were a little bit uncertain going into that meeting initially," Mr. Michael said of the agency's decision to represent Ms. Pejic.

Their strategy for Ms. Pejic is different from the one she pursued as an alternative, androgynous male model. Mr. Michael said the Society instead is hoping to attract "classic American brands like a Donna" (meaning Karan); powerhouse European labels including Céline, Chanel, Fendi, Roberto Cavalli and Prada; and lucrative cosmetics endorsements. He acknowledged that this would potentially require turning down edgier designers and companies that had supported Ms. Pejic in the past.

But will mainstream companies be willing to invest in a transgender woman to represent their brands, on the mostly untested assumption that she will inspire consumers to identify with her, and to spend?

Casting directors seem sanguine about Ms. Pejic's chances. "I think a lot of people would probably be willing," said James Scully, who casts fashion shows for Carolina Herrera, Derek Lam, Jason Wu, Tom Ford and Stella McCartney. "I don't think it would be now so far-fetched, if it really truly were a beautiful girl I could put in front of a client." He paused to add: "Depending on who the client was."

He noted that he was "not aware that she's being marketed this season for show season," and that such conversations would likely have already taken place. (He estimated that shows across the board are 70 percent cast in advance, with 30 percent happening during castings, mostly for new faces.) He guessed that she would appear exclusively for one or a small handful of major houses.

At press time, a representative for the Society was not able to confirm any bookings, citing ongoing discussions.

"I would not rule it out, that's for sure," Mr. Scully said of the likelihood of Ms. Pejic's success. "She could be the Laverne Cox of the modeling world, really get out there and turn the tables." (Ms. Cox is the Emmy-nominated transgender actress and star of "Orange Is the New Black" who appeared on the cover of Time Magazine in June under the headline "The Transgender Tipping Point.")

Ms. Pejic, who said she returned to modeling after her transition in part to be a role model for young trans people, is game to find out.

"It's definitely a different strategy now than it was before," she said. "I want to go for something more classic. To show the world I can be approachable, and not have them think of me as an alien. I feel that for a lot of my career, I had success, I was adored, but I was also this alien creature. I want to show that I have the skill like any other female model, and I'm asking for the same equal treatment and equal respect as any other female model."

Transgender Models Find a Home

BY ALYSON KRUEGER | MARCH 3, 2017

AS ONE OF THE fashion industry's increasing numbers of transgender models, Yasmine Petty has reached great success. Her sprawling penthouse in Lower Manhattan, with a terrace so large it has a pool and cabana, is full of magazines like Elle, W and Hercules that feature multiple-page spreads on her wearing clothing by brands like Marc Jacobs and Louis Vuitton.

Ms. Petty's closet, too, is full of clothes she has modeled at international events like New York Fashion Week, fashion shows put on by Italian Vogue, and Life Ball, Europe's prestigious charity gala to support people with H.I.V. She has walked the runway with stars like Naomi Campbell and Karolina Kurkova. The prominent makeup artist Pat McGrath used her as an "ambassador."

At the beginning of her career Ms. Petty said she worked with several modeling agencies that found her work, but the experience left her feeling somewhat frustrated about the direction her career seemed to be taking.

Some agencies didn't know whether to cast her as male or female, she said. Often she would walk into auditions not knowing which gender she was supposed to perform until she saw the other candidates waiting in the lobby. Other times she would be booked by clients, only to have them find out she was transgender later and refuse to use the photos. "The fashion industry didn't know how to treat me," she said.

Ms. Petty is now so established in her career that she doesn't necessarily need a modeling agency to get new gigs. "I work freelance," she said. But she now has an option for support: Trans Models, perhaps the city's first agency to represent only transgender models.

"They are more familiar representing someone like themselves," she said. "If they would have existed all along, it would have been completely different. I would have walked into a casting knowing I was being represented as myself, and I don't have to hide or be afraid if the client finds out."

Peche Di founded the Trans Models agency two years ago to advance her own modeling career and to help her community.

Trans Models was started in March 2015 by Peche Di, a 27-year-old trans-female who wanted to advance her prospects as a model and help her community. She is working with both established talents like Ms. Petty and newer faces.

A few weeks after her agency opened, she booked a client, Laith Ashley, in a prominent spread in the magazine i-D. She landed the transgender plus-size model Shay Neary a major campaign with Coverstory, a fashion brand. She and two of her clients became the faces of New York City's health campaign for protected sex. "We're on buses," Ms. Di said. "I get texts from my friends saying, 'You're on West Fourth Street.'"

It is no longer unusual, nor a matter of secrecy, to see transgender models on mainstream runways. At the most recent New York Fashion Week, Marc Jacobs employed three: Casil McArthur among the men, and Stav Strashko and Avie Acosta among the women. Vincent Beier walked for Coach and Proenza Schouler.

And while Trans Models may be the first firm of its kind in New York City, similar ones are popping up around the world.

Cecilio Asuncion, the director of "What's the T," a documentary that explored the lives of five transgender women, opened Slay Model Management in Los Angeles last year. Along with walking for New York Fashion Week and Los Angeles Fashion Week, his models have also modeled for Airbnb, Spiegel, even a Brazilian vodka company.

A year ago Mitr Trust, a lesbian, gay, bisexual and transgender charity based in India, held auditions for the country's first transgender modeling agency. As of the end of January, Britain also has its own agency based in Nottinghamshire, England, named Transgender Model U.K. In their first week of operation, they signed two models.

With the attention transgender personalities have received in the press and pop culture in recent years, it's hard to imagine that transgender models are still at a disadvantage. But for many of them, transgender-only agencies are still the only groups that will represent them.

Ms. Di opened Trans Models after spending a decade trying to find an agency to sign her both in Bangkok, where she is from, and in New York. "They would accept a photo, but nothing would happen after," she said. She said reality hit home after she won the transgender pageant Miss Asia New York and modeled for Bruce Weber's "Brothers, Sisters, Sons and Daughters" campaign for Barneys, but still couldn't persuade a firm to sign her.

Mr. Asuncion realized the plight of transgender models after filming his documentary. "I learned that what the community needed was employment," he said. "I figured why not create a space for them?" Even Ms. Petty said she went to about 30 agencies looking for someone to book her at the beginning of her career. "I was turned down by all of them."

Sara Ziff, the founder and executive director of the Model Alliance, a labor advocacy group for models working in the American fashion industry, said this didn't surprise her. "For years the talent pool has been predominantly young, white, tall, thin and female," Ms. Ziff said. "While the industry is slowly evolving and becoming more inclusive, it's difficult for people who don't fit the mold to break in."

Over 300 models have applied to be part of Trans Models; Ms. Di has chosen 19 so far and gets new applicants almost every day. Slay Model management represents 17 models. But while the agencies are popular in this community, it's unclear how much they really can do for clients.

Opportunities for transgender models can be limited, Ms. Di said: "It's still a struggle for our agency to find consistent, paid work for models."

One of her clients, Shane Henise, a 25-year-old transgender man with a handsome but boyish face and giggly personality, has never been booked for a modeling job (he does get television and film gigs). "The options really just aren't there," he said. "When you think about male models, they are very tall and very built, and I'm 5-foot-5 on a good day."

The jobs that do come in are from companies or publications specifically looking for transgender models.

If more and more advertisers want to associate themselves with this community, that is a good thing, said Jack Halberstam, a professor of gender studies at Columbia: "A shift from including transpeople as potential models versus seeing them as completely unthinkable in these roles definitely signifies a sea change in public opinion of trans bodies," Professor Halberstam said. But it isn't the same as transgender models being able to get the same bookings as their peers.

Ms. Ziff said, "A model wants to be booked for a job because she is a great model — not simply because she is black so she ticks that box, or because she is trans so she ticks that box."

Ms. Petty concurred. "Why couldn't I model for Agent Provocateur lingerie or why not Victoria's Secret?" she asked. "Or maybe do cosmetics for Mac or Nars. I'm very optimistic that it could happen, and it's a dream of mine. But it hasn't happened yet."

Mainstream modeling agencies will tell you they also represent transgender models when appropriate. Women Management says it has two star transgender clients: Leandra Medeiros Cerezo, known professionally as Lea T, who was one of the first models to come out as transgender, and Valentina Sampaio, the current cover star of French Vogue. "We only sign clients to Women Management that we think have the merit to succeed in this business, transgender or otherwise," said Michael Bruno, an agent at Women Management. "We work to provide them the same opportunities as other models."

But models seek more from an agency than professional opportunities.

Mr. Henise also gets a sense of belonging from being part of Trans Models. He grew up in a religious household with parents who sent him to strict all-girls schools.

He said the times he spent with the people in the agency conducting photo shoots, talking about their struggles or just hanging out, were the only points in his life he had been with people just like him.

Ms. Di understands what a big deal having a supportive community is for her models, and she is starting additional projects to make their lives richer and easier. With Michael Osofsky, an entrepreneur, she has begun TeaDate, a dating app for transgender people. It started up on Valentine's Day last year with 5,000 users and now has 23,000. Ms. Di is also trying to digitize the fashion booking process by building an app that connects transgender models around the world with work opportunities.

"A lot of times when you first enter a trans community, it is kind of competitive, and you are surrounded by people trying to win over each other," she said. "I'm forming a community within a community that can help each other."

While modeling is often dismissed as superficial, some transgender people consider it a revolutionary act, a means of showing they are just as beautiful and professional as anyone else. "You are not just a model doing your job, superficially having your photo taken," Ms. Petty said. "You are a role model; you are a leader of this movement."

Professor Halberstam is skeptical of this argument, saying: "It's great that there are transbodies visible in the world, but one should be careful about what it means beyond that and about making claims politically. All visibility doesn't all lead in a progressive direction. Sometimes it's just visibility."

Last Night, Calvin Klein — This Morning, Algebra

BY JACOB BERNSTEIN | SEPT. 8, 2017

ARIEL NICHOLSON MURTAGH made her fashion week debut Thursday night walking in Raf Simons's Calvin Klein show. She is 6-foot-1, weighs 125 pounds and has a kind of Pre-Raphaelite-by-way-of-Joni Mitchell hairdo.

So she looks every bit the part of a runway model, even if she's a 16-year-old high school sophomore who also happens to be transgender.

Some may find this a little unseemly. High school sophomores, walking in runway shows, on a school night?

Ah, well. If the fashion industry continues to rely upon teenagers to do adult jobs, why not do it with an eye toward diversity?

Anyway, having been selected by Calvin Klein's designer, Mr. Simons, two weeks after signing with DNA Model Management — the agency that represents Natalia Vodianova, Linda Evangelista and Doutzen Kroes — Ms. Murtagh was stoked to be getting recognized by the industry.

She watched guidance videos of how to walk on YouTube, and could only laugh when members of Mr. Simons's team provided suggestions on how to quickly improve.

"I did it very Victoria's Secret runway," she said, two hours before the Calvin Klein show. A walking, talking exclamation point who reads George Orwell novels in her spare time and also leans in on words such as "like" and "amazing," she was in a bathrobe on the third floor of the company's Midtown Manhattan headquarters.

Their message was clear and correct, she said: "Tone it down."

In her hair were bobby pins, which would be removed at the time of the show.

To her right was her mother, Kerry Murtagh, who works in sales at Benjamin Moore, and would not be removed.

Ariel Nicholson Murtagh was selected by Calvin Klein's designer two weeks after signing with DNA Model Management.

"I know how much school means to her," Kerry Murtagh said. "I don't want her to get crazy."

Almost from the time the younger Ms. Murtagh could speak, she told Kerry and her father, Bob Murtagh, that a boy was not what she was. (The Murtaghs and are now divorced; Kerry lives in Park Ridge, N.J., and Bob lives in Westchester, N.Y.)

She wanted to wear pink tutus and couldn't stop watching "The Little Mermaid." That is the story of an isolated, deep sea princess named Ariel whose body is out of sync with her desire to be fully human.

Kerry got the message quickly, while Bob took a little longer. "I would go by her bed and there were books on her nightstand," Ms. Murtagh said. "Then I'd go to my father's side and there was, like, a drink of water."

In fifth grade, Ms. Murtagh switched pronouns and began taking Lupron, a drug that suppresses the effects of puberty.

The longer she spent living as a girl, the happier she became. Her grades were excellent, Kerry said. Kids at school also seemed to have an easier time accepting a transgender classmate than they did accepting a feminine boy.

"We live in a binary world," Ms. Murtagh said.

In eighth grade, she appeared in "Growing Up Trans," a documentary that was broadcast on PBS stations, in which she talked with her therapist Jean Malpas of the Ackerman Institute about the decision to go on estrogen.

Having made the gender leap early, Ms. Murtagh acclimated quickly.

She no longer has much desire to wear ball gowns and sometimes gets embarrassed telling schoolmates how she selected her name. "So sometimes I say I chose it after Ariel in Shakespeare's 'The Tempest,' " Ms. Murtagh said.

The last movie she loved was "Baby Driver." Her favorite pop star is Lorde, the music world's torchbearer for gritty girl power.

In August, Ms. Murtagh appeared in a Vogue spread devoted to transgender children, wearing a black and white polka dot Giambattista Valli dress with floral detailing, photographed by Inez Van Lamsweerde and Vinoodh Matadin.

"They were so nice," said Ms. Murtagh, who seemed slightly less impressed by the photographers' status at the forefront of fashion photography than their history collaborating with Lady Gaga. "There was a picture of her just, like, on the wall. It was like crazy. I couldn't believe they'd shot people like that!"

Ms. Van Lamsweerde and Mr. Matadin were in the crowd at Calvin Klein Thursday evening as the show began.

Homages to creepy movies prevailed, as battle axes hung from the ceiling and music from David Lynch films played.

Ms. Murtagh came early, and sauntered around the room in a denim and red leather cowboy outfit with a Warhol print emblazoned across the chest. "I actually did a report on Warhol last year for art history!" she said.

Backstage afterward, Ms. Van Lamsweerde proclaimed Ms. Murtagh to be "a natural," and Mr. Simons said she had the right personality for the runway. Which, translated into plain-speak, means that she was every bit as icy and vacant as all the other models in today's fashion-meets-"The Walking Dead" era.

But Ms. Murtagh didn't even get to stay and catch up with any of her new fans, much less Mahershala Ali, the Academy Award winner, whom she spotted out front in the distance.

"Oh my god!" she said, now wearing a floral print Urban Outfitters jacket and American Eagle jeans. "Oh my god! From 'Moonlight'! I'm freaking out!"

Her mother, though, was marveling about how short fashion shows actually are. "Two minutes and then it's over," she said, exaggerating only slightly.

If only they didn't have to leave. If only there wasn't another appearance the following morning to get up for.

"School!" Ms. Murtagh said, walking for the exits.

CHAPTER 2

Artists and Filmmakers

The mid-2010s brought a suite of films featuring stories of transgender characters, from 2015's "The Danish Girl" and "About Ray" to 2016's "Tangerine" and 2017's "A Fantastic Woman." As a result, the film industry has been engaged in a lively debate over the significance and ethics of transgender representations. Can a transgender story be told by a cisgendered writer, director, or actor? What happens when transgender artists are given control over their own stories? In this chapter, filmmakers, writers, and actors explore these questions with reporters.

Who Gets to Play the Transgender Part?

BY BROOKS BARNES | SEPT. 3, 2015

LOS ANGELES — More than at any time in its history, Hollywood is under enormous pressure to find performers who match the racial and ethnic traits of characters.

Ridley Scott was harshly criticized for using non-Egyptian actors to play Egyptians in "Exodus." The director Cameron Crowe faced an online mob for casting Emma Stone as an Asian-American woman in "Aloha." (He ultimately apologized.) When Warner Bros. announced that Rooney Mara would play Tiger Lily in its forthcoming "Pan," the studio was served with a petition headlined "Stop Casting White Actors to Play People of Color!"

But does it remain acceptable — at this Caitlyn Jenner and Laverne Cox moment — for non-transgender actors and actresses to play transgender characters?

Hollywood is about to find out. Two high-profile new films, each with Oscar aspirations, star performers who are not transgender in major transgender roles. On Saturday, "The Danish Girl," with Eddie Redmayne in the title role, will have its world premiere at the Venice Film Festival. "About Ray," starring Elle Fanning as a teenager in early gender transition, arrives next Saturday at the Toronto International Film Festival.

Both casting decisions reflect what remains the dominant view in movies and television. A dozen casting directors, producers, network programmers and studio executives said in interviews that transgender roles were best filled by finding the best actor or actress, regardless of gender identity. In other words, acting is acting. Besides, they asked, don't transgender performers want to be considered for non-transgender roles?

Peter Saraf, a producer of "About Ray," which is to be released in theaters on Sept. 18, said emphatically at the start of an interview that Hollywood needed to work "a lot harder to create opportunities for trans actors to play any kind of role." That said, he defended the casting of Ms. Fanning.

"We try to make the strongest creative choices we can," he said. "Elle, who is one of the most exciting and extraordinary actresses working today, was passionate about the role, and we had the confidence that she could carry a movie."

But some advocates believe that it is flatly offensive for a non-transgender performer to play a transgender part. Jos Truitt, executive director of development at Feministing, an online network, put it this way: When actors like Mr. Redmayne and Jared Leto (who won an Oscar for his portrayal of Rayon in "Dallas Buyers Club") play these roles, it perpetuates "the stereotype that trans women are just men in drag."

At least in some corners of Hollywood, a similar position is gaining steam.

"At this moment in time, especially, I think this industry has a responsibility to put trans actors in trans roles," said Sean Baker, who directed "Tangerine," an independent film that was released in July and starred two transgender actresses. "To not do it seems very wrong in my eyes. There is plenty of trans talent out there."

Adding complexity to the matter, Glaad, which aggressively monitors Hollywood's depictions of gay, lesbian, bisexual and transgender characters, has taken a more nuanced stance. Jeffrey Tambor plays a retired professor beginning a transition on Amazon's "Transparent," and in March that series won a Glaad Media Award, a prize that lists "fair, accurate and inclusive representations" among its criteria.

"There is a consensus that trans actors bring a certain authenticity to a trans role and that trans actors should also have the opportunity to play non-trans characters," said Nick Adams, who leads Glaad's transgender efforts. Beyond that, Mr. Adams said, there is little agreement among advocates, with some supporting Ms. Truitt's hard-line position and others allowing that "in certain circumstances, a non-trans person can play a trans character if they do their homework and learn from trans people, as Jeffrey Tambor did."

For the most part, the transgender stories that Hollywood is telling focus on early transition, perhaps because that process can be mined easily for drama, Mr. Adams noted. That focus also gives studios cover to cast non-transgender performers; Mr. Redmayne must appear as a man at the beginning of "The Danish Girl," for instance. (Glaad is pushing Hollywood to focus less on transition stories.)

Movies like "About Ray" and "The Danish Girl" also face business realities.

"I'm embarrassed to say this, because I do strongly believe that we should be casting transgender performers in these parts — it matters — but often you don't even seriously consider them, because the studio needs a name for financing or marketing reasons," said one leading casting director, speaking on the condition of anonymity because, she said, she considered the topic "radioactive."

Ms. Fanning and Mr. Redmayne were not available for interviews, according to their representatives. None of the filmmakers or studio executives behind "The Danish Girl" would discuss Mr. Redmayne's casting.

"The Danish Girl" is the more high-profile film, in part because it comes from an Academy Award-winning director, Tom Hooper ("The King's Speech"), and stars the reigning best actor; Mr. Redmayne won an Oscar in February for his portrayal of Stephen Hawking in "The Theory of Everything." Mr. Hooper approached Mr. Redmayne for "The Danish Girl" in 2011, when they were working on "Les Misérables."

Mr. Hooper recently told Screen Daily that he sensed "a certain gender fluidity" in Mr. Redmayne. "The Danish Girl," set for release in theaters on Nov. 27 by the Universal-owned Focus Features, tells the true story of a Copenhagen artist who underwent sex reassignment surgery in 1930. It was one of the first such efforts.

In the time it took for "The Danish Girl" to be made, however, transgender issues have leaped to the cultural forefront.

Ms. Cox, the transgender actress who plays Sophia Burset on "Orange Is the New Black," appeared on the cover of Time last year. President Obama in January turned heads by using the word "transgender" in his State of the Union address. "Transparent" won best comedy series in front of 19 million viewers at the last Golden Globe Awards.

And then came Ms. Jenner, who spoke about her transition in a prime-time ABC News special, subsequently posing for the cover of Vanity Fair.

At the same time, pushback on casting decisions large and small has become harder for Hollywood to ignore. Just a few years ago, protests of insensitivity — over the hiring of Johnny Depp to play Tonto in "The Lone Ranger," for instance, or giving Jake Gyllenhaal the lead in "Prince of Persia: The Sands of Time" — were barely blips on the movie industry's radar. But fans, advocacy groups and rank-and-file critics have grown more sophisticated in their use of social media to organize and voice disappointment.

In today's Internet culture, the tendency is to shoot first and ask questions later. Nuance doesn't always matter. Tiger Lily, who exists in the public imagination (and not in a particularly sensitive way) as a Native American woman, was rewritten to be of a nonspecific race, Ms. Mara ultimately explained. "Pan" is scheduled for release on Oct. 9.

Perhaps to get ahead of any blowback, Focus recently had Mr. Redmayne explain to Out magazine how he met with many transgender women to educate himself. "Gosh, it's delicate," he said in that interview. "And complicated."

Part of the frustration with Hollywood among transgender people involves the lack of transgender characters, even with heightened cultural attention. Of the 161 mainstream and art house films that Glaad tracked in its last Studio Responsibility Index, released in April, none had a transgender character. "The list of mainstream films that have depicted transgender people as multifaceted or even recognizable human beings remains tragically short," Glaad wrote in the report.

Television, which moves faster as a business and does not face the same pressure to cast stars, is doing a better job. "Transparent," "Orange Is the New Black" and "Sense8" — notably all from streaming services — prominently feature transgender characters and transgender actors and actresses. Glaad gives particular credit to "The Fosters," an ABC Family series that features the transgender actor Tom Phelan as a transgender teenager.

Glaad is to release a report in November that assesses the television landscape from a transgender perspective. On Thursday, it released its annual Network Responsibility Index, which focuses on "the quantity and quality" of images of gay, lesbian, bisexual and transgender people on television, and used the platform to push for more transgender representation. It told CW, for instance, that it hopes to "see a transgender character make an appearance very soon."

For transgender actors and actresses, that is encouraging — if networks seek them out for any resulting roles.

"Because I am a trans woman in 2015, there are opportunities that wouldn't have existed for me three years ago," said Hari Nef, who will join the cast of "Transparent" when it returns in December. "But Hollywood still seems very wary. There is not a rush of casting agents headed our way. Let's hope that changes. I'm right here!"

Transgender, and Embraced, on the Red Carpet

BY CARA BUCKLEY | DEC. 9, 2015

TWO YEARS AGO, while Jared Leto was busy collecting awards en route to his Oscar win for playing a transgender woman in "Dallas Buyers Club," the independent filmmaker Sean Baker was unwittingly making history shooting "Tangerine."

The story of two transgender besties turning tricks in Hollywood, the film astounded Sundance audiences when they learned it had been shot entirely by iPhone. But what might prove to be the movie's biggest coup came this fall, when an Oscar campaign was started for the film and its stars, Mya Taylor and Kitana Kiki Rodriguez.

While a long shot, it is the first Oscar run for transgender actresses and has already borne fruit: Ms. Taylor won best breakthrough at the Gothams, another first for a transgender actress. The campaign represents a departure from Hollywood's history of celebrating straight or nontransgender actors in Oscar-bait transgender roles. Among them: John Lithgow in "The World According to Garp"; Jaye Davidson in "The Crying Game"; Hilary Swank in "Boys Don't Cry"; Felicity Huffman in "Transamerica"; and Mr. Leto, who played Rayon, a transgender prostitute with AIDS. All were nominated, and two won.

"As remarkable and inspiring as some portrayals of us by cis people have been, they will always be on the outside of our experience," Jennifer Finney Boylan, a transgender writer and activist, said in an email. (Cis is shorthand for cisgender, a term for someone who is not transgender.) "People have fawned over the so-called bravery of cis actors representing what to us is the reality of our daily lives."

In a culture increasingly obsessed with self-obsession, rarely if ever seeing anyone like you on screen, Ms. Boylan said, fosters a dispiriting sense of invisibility.

"There is a big difference between thinking, 'There is someone trying to imitate someone like me,' and 'There is someone like me, on screen, visible, and real,'" she said.

There has been a tidal change for transgender visibility in just the short time since Mr. Leto's Academy win. Laverne Cox graced Time's cover and was nominated for an Emmy for her performance in "Orange Is the New Black"; the Amazon series "Transparent" has won two Golden Globes and five Emmys; Caitlyn Jenner very publicly transitioned; President Obama included the word "transgender" in a State of the Union address.

It was in this newly receptive cultural landscape that Mr. Baker found himself with his movie, as did Tom Hooper, the Academy Award-winning director whose latest film, "The Danish Girl," may be an Oscar candidate (and, truth be told, a more viable one). It tells the true story of Lili Elbe, a turn-of-the-20th-century Danish painter — played by an Oscar winner, Eddie Redmayne — who became one of the first recipients of gender reassignment surgery. (Mr. Redmayne picked up a Screen Actors Guild Award nomination on Wednesday.)

When Mr. Hooper took on the project seven years ago, he was told it would be difficult to finance, cast and distribute. Only after two major successes — "The King's Speech" and "Les Misérables" — was he able to get it off the ground. "I'm now getting people saying it's zeitgeist, it's timely," Mr. Hooper said. "It's quite surreal, because that wasn't the landscape when we started."

Mr. Hooper seems well aware of the increasing pressure to cast transgender actors in transgender roles, but he said he always felt Mr. Redmayne — "he has this raw emotional transparency" — was ideal for Lili. "I think there's something about Eddie that's drawn to the feminine," Mr. Hooper said, noting that Mr. Redmayne played Viola in an all-male production of "Twelfth Night."

Mr. Hooper also cast two transgender actors in cisgender roles: Rebecca Root, who plays Lili's nurse, and Jake Graf, a transgender man who plays a small part. It was the third cisgender role for Ms.

Root, who is one of the leads in the BBC sitcom "Boy Meets Girl," and she is having her busiest acting year yet. Whether to cast a nontransgender or a transgender performer for a character undergoing a transition remained, she said, a "gritty question." She continued: "Who's the right actor in terms of talent, look, voice and indeed public profile? Let's face it, star power is what gets a film financed."

Indeed the gilded credentials of both Mr. Hooper and Mr. Redmayne, who delivers a carefully wrought performance, might draw in otherwise skeptical viewers. Mr. Hooper said that after one screening, the head of a homeless shelter for transgender youth forecast that the film would save lives: Many of her young charges were expelled from families that rejected their gender identities. Ms. Root had pressed upon the film's leads how invaluable her own transition had been. "I was either headed for a mental breakdown, or I was going to commit suicide," she said.

The character of Lili also represents yet another shift from stereotypical depictions of transgender people on screen (which was one of the criticisms levied at Mr. Leto's Rayon), as sex workers, drug addicts, deviants and villains. One transgender woman, who documented her transition on YouTube, said that when she came out, people replied, "Oh, like Buffalo Bill," the murderer in "The Silence of the Lambs" (which nabbed five Oscars) who skinned his female victims to make a "woman suit."

While the leads in "Tangerine" play sex workers, their gender identities are a fact of life — which for them is a tough life — but not the film's focus. Ms. Cox, of "Orange Is the New Black," has promoted the film's awards run and was struck by a scene showing a cabdriver's dismay after realizing the sex worker he had picked up was a nontransgender woman. "In so many narratives we see trans people being rejected," she said. "Here we see someone looking for, wanting, desiring a trans woman, which is so rare. There are men who want us."

(The Armenian actor Karren Karagulian, who played the cabby, has weathered vicious backlash from other Armenians for that part.)

Since the film wrapped, Ms. Taylor — who, along with Ms. Rodriguez, met Mr. Baker at a Hollywood center for lesbian, bisexual and transgender clients while he was researching the film — has moved to North Dakota to be with her fiancé. The role in "Tangerine" has changed her life, and she frequently travels to Los Angeles for work and auditions. (Mr. Baker said Ms. Rodriguez decided to no longer be part of the awards campaign because she is considering a career in counseling.)

Ms. Taylor now finds herself in a position similar to Ms. Cox, as a spokeswoman for transgender people, appreciative of the increased visibility yet dismayed at the soaring rates of homicide, suicide attempts and unemployment that plague this world. "Visibility is very important, but it's not changing the day-to-day lives of everyday trans people," Ms. Cox said. "We need another culture shift."

Last month, Ms. Taylor was invited to a White House event honoring lesbian, gay, bisexual and transgender artists, and attended a panel about "inclusive storytelling." Moderated by Raffi Freedman-Gurspan, the White House's first transgender staff member, the speakers included Jill Soloway, who created "Transparent"; Jeffrey Tambor, its star; and Rhys Ernst, a transgender filmmaker and artist.

Sitting in the audience, Ms. Taylor ran through all the things she would have talked about had she been asked to speak.

"Of course everything is great for me," Ms. Taylor said. "But I think about the other people who were in the position that I was in, like being homeless, and prostituting. They're still doing that same thing. I think about that."

The Star of 'A Fantastic Woman' Picks a Few Come-Hither Dresses

BY RUTH LA FERLA | FEB. 1, 2018

DANIELA VEGA glanced appraisingly into the makeup mirror. Her eyelids, slicked with gloss by a tirelessly hovering makeup artist, gave her the humid, come-hither look of a 1930s cinema vamp. Pretty much as she'd planned.

"I want to look like a period piece," said Ms. Vega, the 28-year-old Chilean star of "A Fantastic Woman." Ms. Vega, a transgender actress who plays a passably stylish transgender woman in the film (a contender for the Best Foreign Language Oscar), acknowledged that, on screen or off, fashion has long been a formidable tool in her arsenal.

She was prepping last week in her gray-on-gray suite at the strenuously modish Langham Hotel in the southern part of Midtown Manhattan, riffling through her outsize closet in anticipation of the multicity tour promoting the movie's release. (It opens nationally on Feb. 2.) She would be visiting Washington the next morning, followed in whirlwind succession by Tokyo, Madrid and, within a brief span of days, New York again.

She wasn't complaining. Dressing for an imagined public is, to her mind, a performance.

"Life is a 'pasarela,' a runway," she said. Switching gamely between her native Spanish and occasional bursts of un-self-conscious English, she added, "You can shine or be low key. I always prefer to get attention."

That craving persists. When Ms. Vega transitioned at 17, she rejoiced privately. "At the time, I told myself, 'Now I can wear whatever I want,'" she said.

She does. Her options last week included the spangled black georgette gown she wore on the red carpet last month at the Golden Globes where "A Fantastic Woman" had been nominated for best foreign

Daniela Vega, who stars in "A Fantastic Woman," puts on makeup in her hotel suite in New York.

language film. She let its hem trail, its gossamer fabric contrasting zanily with her white canvas sneakers.

Those shoes were a backup. Some 20 pairs of stiletto-heeled pumps, including her favorite — a cream-colored pair with a pointy, black-tipped toe — were lost for the moment in transit. "They were my babies," she said.

Not given to prolonged mourning, she turned to a lavishly pleated, ankle-grazing green velvet dress, plucked it off the rack, clutched it to her chest and gave it the girlish twirl of a 1950s ingénue. "I love to wear velvet," she crooned. "It makes me feel like a person in a different century."

She was carrying on for her audience, a retinue that included a translator, the movie's publicist and her makeup artist, a reassuring sidekick on Ms. Vega's travels. Her guests cheered her on as she slipped a pale silk damask coat over her black utility jeans. "Feel this

fabric — it's so heavy," she said, gazing back over her shoulder with the glassy hauteur of a society swan.

"This piece is very '60s, very Jackie Kennedy style. I'll wear it to the Critics' Choice awards," Ms. Vega said, weighing every one of her looks for its potential to turn heads.

She has had plenty of practice. Hers may not be a household name, but her image, looming larger than life on billboards in her native Santiago, where she is the face of a shopping mall and a fashionable eyewear brand, has lent her a demi-celebrity.

"It's not like I wake up in the morning and tell myself I'm famous," she said. "Madonna is famous. But when I look up from the back seat of a taxi and see my face 40 feet high, that's when I remember I'm a star."

In Manhattan, she is recognized only rarely. "Some guys look at me and wink, very flirtatiously," she said. "Women tell me, 'I like your coat, where did you get it?' "

Her star turn in "A Fantastic Woman" as Marina, a nightclub singer and waitress in Santiago whose older lover, Orlando, virtually dies in her arms, is likely to broaden her fan base. Ms. Vega brought warmth and grit to a role of a woman facing, in the aftermath of her lover's collapse, chilling hostility, humiliation and bouts of physical aggression from his family and the local authorities, who treat her with contempt.

The role, she said, helped her channel her defiance. "Marina has been built on three basic pillars," she said. "The first one is dignity. The second is rebellion, and the third is resilience."

Chile is not notably supportive of trans people, but Ms. Vega finds refuge in her work. "No one programmed that I was going to be an actress," she said. "But it was the place where I felt comfortable."

Coming out to her family was daunting. At 14, she told her parents, " 'I think that my body is giving me a message,' " she said. " 'I'm not going to walk in the road that was assigned to me.' "

Her parents spent a weekend sorting out their feelings. On their return they presented her with a box. She thought it held passes to see a psychiatrist. "But it was a makeup box. They gave it to me and said,

'Welcome,' " Ms. Vega said, her eyes misting. "I still have it. I keep my rings there."

She wore no rings in her hotel suite the other day, her jewel-free look in keeping with a sober turn in the conversation. She was uncertain of the reception she would find in the United States, keenly aware of a sociopolitical climate that can be hostile to outliers.

"But I feel that the world is progressive in spite of the power that very few people have to make you believe the opposite," she said. "You may believe that a statue is talking to you, but of course it's not. There is a very fine line between what you believe and what is really happening."

"That line divides people," she said. "That's where the danger lies."

Does she feel that danger personally?

Ms. Vega considered the question for a beat, her features darkening.

"I am afraid of death," she said finally. "But in life, I'm not afraid of anyone."

Second Wachowski Sibling Comes Out as Transgender Woman

BY LIAM STACK | MARCH 9, 2016

A SECOND SIBLING from the film-directing duo that created "The Matrix" series came out as a transgender woman on Tuesday after a reporter from The Daily Mail appeared on her front porch to ask questions about her gender identity.

The director, Lilly Wachowski — who with her sister, Lana, are the first major Hollywood directors to come out as transgender — condemned the British publication for sending the reporter to her home on Monday night and released her own statement to The Windy City Times in Chicago.

"I knew at some point I would have to come out publicly," she wrote. "You know, when you're living as an out transgender person it's … kind of difficult to hide. I just wanted — needed some time to get my head right, to feel comfortable. But apparently I don't get to decide this."

Ms. Wachowski thanked friends and family for their support, saying it had given her "the chance to actually survive this process."

With her announcement, Ms. Wachowski, previously known as Andy, joined a growing list of openly transgender people in Hollywood, including her sister and filmmaking partner, who was known as Larry before coming out in 2012; the reality stars Caitlyn Jenner and Chaz Bono; the writer and musician Our Lady J; and the actresses Laverne Cox, Alexandra Billings, Trace Lysette and Hari Nef.

The Wachowskis created "The Matrix" films before transitioning, and have collaborated on a number of other high-profile projects over the past two decades, usually works of science fiction that include a lesbian, gay, bisexual or transgender element, including "Bound," "V for Vendetta," "Jupiter Ascending" and the Netflix series "Sense8."

Lilly Wachowski recounted the exchange with The Daily Mail reporter in her statement to The Windy City Times, saying that he told her she "had to sit down with him" to tell her "inspirational" story and to have her picture taken — adding that she "didn't want to have someone from The National Enquirer following me around, did I?"

In a statement Wednesday, The Daily Mail said it "categorically denies" trying to "coerce" Ms. Wachowski into revealing her transgender identity.

"Our reporter was extremely sympathetic and courteous at all times" a spokesman for DailyMail.com said, referring to an unreleased transcript of the conversation with the director.

"We wish Lilly Wachowski well with her journey, though we are surprised as to how she has reacted, given the courtesy and sensitivity with which the reporter approached her," he added.

The Daily Mail was harshly criticized for its handling of transgender issues after it ran a column about Lucy Meadows, a British teacher who transitioned over Christmas break in 2012, under the headline "He's not only in the wrong body … he's in the wrong job."

Ms. Meadows killed herself three months later, citing debts, job stress and the recent death of loved ones, according to The Guardian. But the coroner in Lancashire, England, condemned the news media after her death and singled out The Daily Mail for what he called its "character assassination" and "ridicule and humiliation" of a private citizen.

In its statement, Wednesday, The Daily Mail rejected the argument that its coverage had played any role in the death of Ms. Meadows.

Ms. Wachowski said Monday was not the first time that she had been approached by a reporter.

Her agent called several times over the past year to tell her a media outlet was about to publish an article on her gender transition and had requested a comment, she said.

She prepared a "mega-sarcastic" statement to release in the event that a publication wrote about her transition without her consent, Ms. Wachowski said, but each time, the media outlet backed down.

"And now here they were, at my front door, almost as if to say — 'There's another one! Let's drag 'em out in the open so we can all have a look!' " Ms. Wachowski wrote about her exchange with The Daily Mail reporter.

Transgender people in the United States face far higher rates of murder, poverty and unemployment than the rest of the population, and in the past year several states have considered laws that would make it illegal for a transgender person to use a public restroom that fits his or her gender.

Ms. Wachowski said she hoped the decision by other news media outlets to decline to publish articles before she came out reflected a growing awareness of the "potentially fatal effect" of publicly outing someone.

Faced with a reporter on her doorstep, however, she decided to take control of the information herself, she said.

"So yeah, I'm transgender," she wrote. "And yeah, I've transitioned."

An Oscar-Nominated Transgender Director on His 'Authentic Self'

BY CARA BUCKLEY | FEB. 20, 2018

YANCE FORD is the first transgender director to receive an Oscar nomination, for his documentary "Strong Island." The film is a brutal, intimate portrait of the unraveling of his tight-knit family following the death of his brother, William Ford Jr., in Suffolk County, Long Island, in 1992, and an all-white grand jury's decision to not indict the white man who shot him.

While Mr. Ford was a somber, deeply sorrowful presence in the film, he flipped out when the Oscar nominations were announced; we know this because he recorded his gleeful reaction and it made the local news. I recently spoke with him about how the film has helped shift his lifelong grief, and his hope that other transgender people will be more accepted as a result of his nomination. Here are excerpts from our phone chat this month.

Q. *What kind of feedback are you getting to the film?*

A. I'm hearing from people who were former students of my mother at Thomas Jefferson High School in East New York in the '70s and '80s [where she was the principal], and from school at Rikers [where she started a school for women]. I'm hearing from people who were friends of my brother in high school who didn't realize he was dead. Friends of mine from elementary school and high school.

Netflix opened the door for the rest of the world to see the movie. It just so happened the rest of the world includes people who have written to say my mother changed their lives. People saying yes, thank you for showing that this is not something that black people have been imagining. It's really humbling.

Yance Ford, the director of the documentary "Strong Island."

Q. *I interviewed you this past summer, and now you sound so much lighter, less burdened.*

A. "Strong Island" has been doing more and more of the work. I think that's the shift you hear in my voice. That I haven't been the one to have to carry it all. It's out in the world and can speak for itself. It does take the pressure off me in a way. I definitely feel like I'm more present than the 1992 Yance or the 2012 Yance, when I walked away from a very stable job into what felt like a great unknown. Being out as a trans man isn't new in my personal life, but it's new in the public sphere. I started part of my transition before the film was complete, and now I'm further along in my transition. I'm also more comfortable in my skin. The past 10 years has been about the movie, the movie, the movie. And then I get to be in the world as my authentic self. I think that's the lightness that you hear.

Q. *How does it feel to be so inspiring for people?*

A. I have been gender nonconforming my entire life. One of the things I discovered last year was my brother knew that I was gay, and he had told all of my friends, "Listen Yance is gay, and off limits. I'm taking Yance to everything, prom, this thing, that thing." It reaffirms that my brother saw me for who I was. I can with this nomination remind people that trans people in general and trans people of color in particular are subject to violence at higher rates than most any other group. There was just an article about how trans women feel targeted by the N.Y.P.D., and were assumed to be engaged in sex work. If my nomination helps people at all think about the transgender folks in their lives, in their communities, and treating them as humans and equals deserving of protection, I'm happy.

Q. *Have you heard any reaction from law enforcement in Suffolk County?*

A. Suffolk County criminal justice is in disarray. [Its former police chief is in prison, convicted in 2016 of conspiring to obstruct justice among other charges. The former district attorney faces charges of trying to derail a federal investigation.] I haven't heard a peep, and I honestly didn't expect to. One thing I learned in making the film is that the people involved think they asked all the questions. They think they're right. This is what happens with not having a mechanism for review of the grand jury system, when you have a system that assumes every decision is correct, that doesn't include a mechanism for review no matter how many studies reveal racial bias.

Q. *Does the film's release and success ease the weight of your grief, or change it at all?*

A. Grief for me is a moment-to-moment experience. I wish my parents were here to see it. I wish my mother were here to see this because she participated in the film. I have a lot of surrogate parents, but there's no one like your mother. At the Gotham Awards they played a clip of my mom; it was incredible. The entire room came to a standstill. It was amazing to see the effect my mother has on people. On the other hand, it really magnifies how absent she is.

Q. *Was the name "Strong Island" a metaphor for your family?*

A. "Strong Island" [was temporary] because it was slang for Long Island and I needed a title for my first grant application. Then it became known as that in the doc community. You realize you can't change the title. In hindsight I'm glad I chose it, though it wasn't a metaphor for my family. It helped the people locate the story and keep the title short. I wish it was a little higher in alphabet so I wouldn't have had a heart attack when they announced the nominations.

To Play Transgender, Sandra Caldwell Had to Open Up About Who She Is

BY SOPHIE HAIGNEY | AUG. 28, 2017

IT WASN'T SANDRA CALDWELL'S first audition. By the time she came in to read for the part of Mama Darleena in Philip Dawkins's drama "Charm," Ms. Caldwell had been in dozens of films, television shows, musicals and plays. She'd performed at the Moulin Rouge in Paris, played a small part in Maya Angelou's "Down in the Delta" and had a role in the BET mini-series "The Book of Negroes."

But she was shaking when it was time to read for a part for "Charm," an MCC Theater production that begins previews performances Off Broadway on Thursday.

"My soul was jumping out the window," she said recently. She smiled broadly and shook her head as she retold the story. "I had no idea what was going to happen."

It wasn't her first audition, but it was her first time auditioning as an openly transgender woman. And she was reading for a role that tracked so closely with her personal narrative, she said, that "the monologue in the middle, I could have taken her name off and put my name in."

Like her, Mama Darleena — based on a real person named Gloria Allen — is a black transgender woman in her 60s. Unlike her, Mama Darleena had been openly trans-identifying since her transition. At 65, Ms. Caldwell was ready to open up.

The show's casting director, Adam Caldwell, could tell she was nervous. (They are not related.) But he was struck by her energy and charisma, and how exactly she matched the description of the character. He and MCC had been struggling to cast the part for months.

He sent a message to William Cantler, an artistic director of the theater: "I think you should come to Studio 6." Mr. Cantler did. After a work session with the director, Will Davis, and a callback — in which,

Mr. Cantler said, Ms. Caldwell "took control of that room" — they offered her the part. She burst into tears. So did Mr. Dawkins.

Now in rehearsal, Ms. Caldwell has largely worked through those initial nerves. Her stage presence is powerful: On a recent afternoon, after a successful run-through of a tense early scene, she did a full-body dance around the perimeter of the room, then pumped a fist.

"She's working so hard," Mr. Davis said. "She really wants to get this right."

"Charm" follows a crew of teenagers and 20-somethings from wildly different backgrounds who attend etiquette classes at an L.G.B.T.Q. youth center in Chicago, taught by Mama Darleena. Many of the characters are transgender, and Mr. Davis, who is trans-identifying, felt strongly that the parts went to people whose gender identities matched the roles.

In a theater world where jobs still remain heavily white and male, it is not surprising that parts for trans-identifying actors are limited. In his experience, Mr. Davis said, theaters often give familiar reasons for not casting actors from historically marginalized groups: "The same two things get said: 'One, I can't find them; two, they're not trained.' So I feel very, very strongly that it's actually the responsibility of the institution to find and train them."

MCC used nontraditional methods to find actors for the nine-member cast. They put out a call on social media, tried networking through friends, and reached out to lesbian and gay youth centers and organizations. They tried to cast a net well beyond New York City and Los Angeles.

Mama Darleena was a particular challenge. "The fact that a trans woman of color in her 60s is alive is a miracle in and of itself because of the oppressive ways that that group of people has been treated in the last 60 years," Mr. Davis said. "The idea that then on top of that, that person was an actor was a really tall order."

In the 2015 world premiere of "Charm" in Chicago, Mama Darleena was played by a cisgender, or gender conforming, man — though in three other productions, she has been played by transgender women.

Ms. Caldwell was born in Washington but ran away to New York several times, beginning when she was 13 — her way, she said, of "figuring things out." When she was 18, she bought a $6 ticket to a Broadway show. "I didn't know what it was, I just saw the lights," Ms. Caldwell said. It turned out to be the Stephen Sondheim musical "Follies," starring the original cast. "I knew right then that this was what I wanted to do," she said.

She completed her transition around the age of 19. Her mother, with the help of two friends who were involved with L.G.B.T.Q. issues, brought her to counseling and psychiatrists before she received hormone therapy. Afterward, Ms. Caldwell said, "I felt a lot of joy, and also relief."

"Back then," she added "the rules were, you did what you had to do and kept your mouth shut." Outside of her family, only a small group of friends from Washington who had known her as a child were aware of her transition.

She auditioned for a role as a showgirl in New York — and ultimately traveled to Europe and worked at the Moulin Rouge. She had success as an actress. She wrote a one-woman show seven years ago about her life and travels, "The Guide to Being Fabulous After You've Skinned Your Knee," and performed it at Berkeley Street Theater in Toronto, where she lived for over a decade.

But she never mentioned her transition. After that show, "the bottom fell out because I felt like I was lying," she said. "I had left myself out. I left the truth about me out."

Eventually, Ms. Caldwell said, she came to a conclusion: She wanted to start sharing that truth with the world.

About a year ago, she approached Alicia Jeffery, her manager of 14 years. Ms. Caldwell confessed to her that she had transitioned many years ago and was ready to share that with the world.

"I had absolutely no idea," Ms. Jeffery said. "She was known around Toronto to be this very foxy, sexy actress and singer. Which is what she is." They discussed how she might rework her one-woman play to include her transition, and how she might begin to share her story publicly.

Shortly after, Ms. Jeffery saw a casting call for "Charm," and the description of Mama Darleena. She asked Ms. Caldwell if she wanted to be submitted for the part, and Ms. Caldwell said yes. "Well, here we go," Ms. Caldwell recalled saying.

Ms. Caldwell said that she was drawn to the play partly because it wasn't a tragedy. "Some movies with a trans theme — not so much anymore — but they always used to start with somebody being beat up," she said. "Or somebody being hurt. This has nothing to do with that whatsoever. All it touches is this woman who has a gift, a skill to help these folks along."

Ms. Allen, on whom the Mama Darleena character is based, is 72 and still lives in Chicago. She no longer teaches etiquette classes, but she recently flew to New York to meet the cast of "Charm."

Of Ms. Caldwell, she said, "I met her and I fell in love with her right then and there because she is so down to earth and so classy, and I said 'O.K., I see myself in her.'" They've become friends.

Ms. Caldwell knows that once the play opens on Sept. 18, much more may change for her. This is the first time she is sharing the story of her transition in an interview.

"I don't know what it's going to be like," she said. "But I kind of want to live the rest of what I've got on this planet as if there's such a thing as complete freedom. I want to live in that."

Transgender Playwrights: 'We Should Get to Tell Our Own Stories First'

BY ALEXIS SOLOSKI | NOV. 9, 2016

"I WOULD LOVE to see more trans stories by trans people in every theater," the playwright MJ Kaufman said. "That'd be great."

Kaufman, a transgender writer who foregoes honorifics like Mr. or Ms., just might get that chance. The playwright uttered that wish while sitting in an atrium across the street from Lincoln Center on a recent weekday morning, drinking coffee and noshing on a blueberry pastry. Also present for a discussion of gender and performance were Basil Kreimendahl and Jess Barbagallo, two other transgender playwrights.

Mr. Barbagallo's "My Old Man (And Other Stories)," which Time Out called "rich — in swagger, invention, mischief and heat," recently finished a run at Dixon Place. Kaufman's "Sagittarius Ponderosa," produced by the National Asian American Theater Company, continues at 3LD Art & Technology Center until Nov. 19. "Orange Julius," produced by Rattlestick Playwrights Theater and Page 73, will open in January. It will star Mr. Barbagallo as Nut, the transgender child of a Vietnam veteran.

They all knew one another from new-play development circles. (As Kaufman said to Mr. Barbagallo, who is also a performer, "I tried to get you to be in three readings, but you were always busy!") And they are part of a larger community of transgender and gender-fluid theater artists, an ever-growing group that includes Taylor Mac ("Hir"); Sylvan Oswald ("Sex Play," the web series "Outtakes"); Olivia Dufault ("Year of the Rooster"); and writer-performers like Becca Blackwell, Shakina Nayfack and Justin Vivian Bond.

These three writers have a lot in common. All are in their 30s, all wear their hair long on top and short on the sides, all are interested in questions of gender and sexuality while trusting that their writing

From left, the playwrights MJ Kaufman, Basil Kreimendahl and Jess Barbagallo, at Lincoln Center.

ventures beyond those concerns. And all were careful to emphasize that as white transmasculine writers, they did not presume to speak for all transgender artists.

But they work in different styles — Kreimendahl's is visceral, Kaufman's meditative, Mr. Barbagallo's impish. And they have markedly different feelings toward the professional theater and its attitudes toward transgender artists. Kaufman described it as "really, really, really not trans friendly right now." Kreimendahl viewed it, despite the occasional pronoun and bathroom confusion, as a more welcoming place, "very willing to learn and grow, as I am growing into myself." These are edited excerpts from the conversation.

Q. *Can you tell me something about your recent plays?*

Jess Barbagallo It's structured like a collection of short stories. The activity circulates around this guy named Barry and a neighbor who lives in the same apartment complex. It's pretty unwieldy.

MJ Kaufman Mine is about a transmasculine person. His family thinks of him as Angela. But to himself and to his friends, he's mostly Archer. I won't spoil it, but yes, he has to negotiate these two different gender spaces and also a family transition.

Basil Kreimendahl "Orange Julius" is about the relationship between a transmasculine child and their father. I knew I wanted to write about Agent Orange and the stories of children of Vietnam vets, about how Vietnam affects them.

Q. *When did you become interested in playwriting?*

Barbagallo I've been writing since I was in high school. I was surprised to get into a conservatory acting program. I didn't think I was a very good actor. Scene study did leave me a little cold. I graduated from school and then after I was out for a year, I was like, I can't handle my student loans. I'm going to go back to college to become a teacher and I'll study playwriting.

Kreimendahl Like Jess, I always wrote growing up. I wanted to write films. My family, we never went to the theater. I was at a community college in Florida and I took a theater class and a film class. In film class, we just talked about directors. In the theater class, we talked about the playwrights. I was like, I'm doing the wrong thing.

Kaufman I always was into theater and writing. I wrote my first play in a high school drama class. And then I tried to do a lot of other things. I graduated from college and was doing all kinds of weird jobs and I was like, I think I want to be a playwright.

Barbagallo What weird jobs?

Kaufman I was a Spanish teacher and a nanny and a barista.

Kreimendahl I did construction, remodeling.

Barbagallo I was a bartender, I taught school. I work at a magazine now, "Us Weekly." I'm a researcher.

Q. *What were your early plays about?*

Kreimendahl A kid who had a webcam show and who was cyber-bullied and who killed himself live on the webcam. It was a dark comedy.

Barbagallo I was doing a really haphazard Marie Kondo of my apartment and I found a play I wrote when I was 16 or 17. The tone is like a skewed sitcom, like Edward Albee if he wrote plays when he was three.

Kaufman "Shatter" was about a mad scientist who made a computer program to put together every combination of sounds and notes in the world so that no one could ever write new music again.

Q. *And when did your birth gender start to feel uncomfortable?*

Barbagallo From puberty. But I had no way to talk about it. I used to hide myself in lots of layers of clothing. And then when I was in college, I had the classic hair-cutting moment. All of a sudden my teachers were more interested in me. I started getting cast in stuff. I started dating a lot more.

Kaufman I definitely took a really, really long time to choose trans as a label. It was after multiple years of trying out a different pronoun with friends that I was like, I think I could demand that the world respect me this way. That was when I was in grad school. I had a different name then. I started introducing myself as MJ.

Barbagallo Only my mother still calls me by my birth name. My parents knew that I had top surgery, but we don't put the specific language on it.

Kreimendahl I've been Basil for 11 years. I guess because my birth name is so feminine it never felt right. My mom still calls me it. I'm not really out to my parents either. It's not a topic of conversation. But I think that's going to happen soon. I'm about to get married. We don't want this confusion when I'm the groom.

Q. *Are you out to your parents, MJ?*

Kaufman My moms are lesbian, so they definitely have a reference point when I came out to them. They are very supportive in their own way.

Barbagallo You're so lucky.

Q. *Do you have concerns about being pigeonholed as a trans playwright?*

Barbagallo I don't like being tokenized or feeling that other parts of my person are overshadowed. Sometimes when people are asking me to speak on a panel or to come lecture, I'm like, come see my play. Come see the art.

Kaufman That happens to me a lot, too. They'll see my work and the only thing they'll have to say is, "It's so exciting you're writing a trans story. It's so great to see queer and trans characters." Can you say one thing about craft?

Kreimendahl I hope I'm seen as a playwright. I move in the world that way. I don't feel like Rattlestick is doing "Orange Julius" because I'm trans. In San Francisco, they did market my play "Sidewinders" as very queer and the play was not about that. It was about being human. So people came expecting to see a trans narrative and then were disappointed.

Q. *How strong are the autobiographical elements in what you write?*

Kreimendahl "Orange Julius" is the most personal play I've ever written.

Barbagallo In early plays I wrote I was the protagonist, plays about a screwed up 20-something. But as the years have gone on, I am so much less interesting to myself.

Kaufman There's some of myself in all of my work. I have noticed recently that I have a number of plays where there's a transmasculine person with a dead father.

Q. *None of you has written a traditional trans coming-out narrative. Do those stories interest you?*

Kreimendahl Nooo. I've never been interested in the coming-out narrative at all. There's so much more to write about.

Kaufman I do think that one of the reasons I resisted the trans label for so long was the only way I had encountered it was the story of someone who is born in the wrong body and then they get surgery and they take hormones and they transition and then they've found themselves. That's not true for me and for most of the trans people I know.

Q. *You've all written gender nonconforming characters. Is it important to you that gender nonconforming actors play those roles?*

Barbagallo Trans roles, roles specifically for trans people, should be played by trans actors. That's pretty simple.

Kaufman Definitely. Though I am trying to push the conversation away from this authenticity bias of who can do the role most realistically and toward a labor justice question of who's getting cast and who's not. Trans actors have a harder time getting cast even in trans roles and this shouldn't be true.

Kreimendahl We have enough actors out there. It's worth reaching out, outside the normal ways of casting.

Barbagallo I've been asked to come in and read for trans women. I think that might be just about the worst casting choice you could make. There are really gifted performers working who have not necessarily been through conservatory training who could strengthen the fabric of our theater if you reached out to them.

Q. *How do you feel about transgender narratives written by people who aren't transgender?*

Barbagallo Ooh! It's hot right now!

Kreimendahl There's something that just goes, that's not really my story, that's a straight version of my story.

Kaufman I don't see very many cis writers writing about trans experience responsibly. I would love to see that. There's an unfortunate compounding problem that theaters would rather produce work about us, not by us right now. We should get to tell our own stories first.

Our Lady J Evolves, One Dolly Parton Cover at a Time

BY MICHAEL MUSTO | DEC. 10, 2014

THE TRANSGENDER PERFORMER Our Lady J keeps evolving.

She first burst onto the scene as a culty cabaret singer who paid homage to Dolly Parton. "She was one of the top icons in my life as a kid," said Our Lady J, who is 6-foot-1 and cuts a striking glamazon figure.

She is also a trained pianist who has played for such diverse acts as Sia, Lady Gaga and the American Ballet Theater, and who has along the way befriended a number of celebrities, big and small, including Daniel Radcliffe of Harry Potter fame.

And recently, she was hired by the TV director and writer Jill Soloway to be a writer for "Transparent," an Amazon original series about a retired professor, played by Jeffrey Tambor, who is transitioning from male to female.

"I will draw on my own experience," Our Lady J said. "The world is beginning to see us as we've seen ourselves."

Our Lady J's own story could rival that of any Dolly Parton song. Born Justin Spidel into a Pentecostal family in the predominantly Amish town of Edenville, Pa., population around 200, she spent her youth adrift.

"There weren't any kids my age that I could relate to, so I was on the farm with my brothers, which is why I played the piano. I was just bored out of my mind," she said.

"It wasn't until I moved to New York in 2000 that I met trans people and began to see myself in other trans women," she added.

Her career was awakening, too. Shortly after arriving in New York, she freelanced as an accompanist for various arts organizations, including the Alvin Ailey American Dance Theater, Mark Morris's dance troupe and the American Ballet Theater. In 2004, she became

The transgender performer Our Lady J posed at Rockwell Table & Stage in Los Angeles, where she sometimes has shows.

the musical director and accompanist for the ebullient Broadway performer Natalie Joy Johnson, and began gussying up for the part.

"I was dressing female a lot, but I'd never done it onstage," Our Lady J said. "She gave me an opportunity. My favorite outfit was a smart pantsuit with a sensible heel, hair shellacked and face beat for the gods. I'd started calling myself 'Jonnah,' but I decided I needed to come up with another name for the stage."

As a nod to Jean Genet's subversive debut novel, "Our Lady of the Flowers," she adopted "Our Lady" and added the "J" for Justin/Jonnah.

That same year, she accompanied another name changer, Stefani Germanotta — the future pop superstar Lady Gaga — at the CAP21 musical-theater conservatory in New York, where she played piano in Gaga's ballet class and coached vocal techniques. "I hung out with her in L.A. a year ago," Our Lady J said, "and we had a laugh about both of our transitions."

As she came into herself, Our Lady J was developing a fan base of her own, doing her first solo show at the Duplex in Greenwich Village, followed by gigs at Ars Nova and the since-shuttered Zipper Factory, both in Hell's Kitchen. That's where she first did the Dolly Parton show, mixing the country star's gospel hits with her own brooding and whimsical works.

Sitting at the piano, she's hypnotic and often very wry. "I only sing to give words to the story the piano is telling," she said. "Life has been absurd and funny and ridiculous and sad and hard, and I just try to bring all of that to the stage." (She is reprising the show on Dec. 22 at Joe's Pub, accompanied by the Train-To-Kill Gospel Choir.)

She has been doing versions of this show since 2007, and in 2009, Ms. Parton herself arranged a meeting. Our Lady J originally thought Ms. Parton was going to hand her a cease-and-desist order. "But when I realized she just wanted to thank me for singing her songs, her legend became real to me," she said.

Another unlikely fan was Mr. Radcliffe, whom she met through a mutual friend. "He's just a nice kid," said Our Lady J. But tabloid speculation about whether she was dating Mr. Radcliffe turned ugly. "That actually ruined my life for a second," she said. Harry Potter fans wrongly assumed they were an item and made nasty comments on Twitter, Facebook and YouTube. "It was schoolyard stuff all over again. I had to go into therapy after that."

Fortunately, she recovered and kept evolving. In 2009, when she wanted to raise money for breast implants, she turned to her performance peers and put on a fund-raising concert. Taylor Mac, the Scissor Sisters and others performed breast-related songs at the Wild Project theater in the East Village. She raised $10,000.

The singer also wants to have facial feminization surgery, but nothing else. "I'm comfortable being a bit of both genders," she said. "Legally, I'm 100 percent woman — I changed the 'M' to 'F' on all my papers — but now I want to change it to a question mark or an 'X'."

Her willful ambiguity seems to make sense in Los Angeles, where she moved in 2010 for "the sunshine and the silicone," and where she doesn't garner the stares she attracts in New York. "All the Beverly Hills wives look like gorgeous transsexuals," she said. "L.A. is post-gender in that way. You can't tell who was born what."

Meet Jaimie Wilson, a Transgender Activist With Guitar in Hand

BY ALEX HAWGOOD | JAN. 26, 2018

Name Jaimie Wilson

Age 22

Hometown Howell, Mich.

Now Lives in a two-bedroom apartment in the East Village of Manhattan that he shares with a roommate.

Claim to Fame Mr. Wilson is a budding folk-pop musician and baby-faced model who appears on the most recent cover of Candy magazine, as well as in advertisements for the skimpy men's underwear brand 2(x)ist. He is also something of an L.G.B.T. activist by being a plainly outspoken transgender man to his hundreds of thousands of followers on Facebook and Instagram. "Music has the power to bring people outside of the community into the community," he said.

Big Break In March, about one year after he began transitioning, Mr. Wilson posted before-and-after photos (some shirtless) on Facebook that racked up 13 million views. The actress Ruby Rose commented that he was "looking like a young Channing Tatum." The rapper Lil Wayne wrote, "Wow." "People didn't start listening to my music until after my transition, which is funny because I had to really practice to regain my singing voice because my vocal cords had changed so drastically," Mr. Wilson said.

Latest Project In 2015, he started a clothing swap program in Michigan for transitioning men and women called T Is for Trans. But like most New Yorkers with small closets, he had to close up shop when he moved to the city. He still does the occasional giveaway of chest binders (compression garments that reduce the appearance of female

Jaimie Wilson, a baby-faced model, is a budding folk-pop musician.

breasts) through Instagram Stories. "Clothing is the last thing you want to think about when you're spending most of your money on hormones and top surgery funds," he said.

Next Thing In February he will release his first EP, funded on Kickstarter, "Life Is a Journey." After playing at last year's Sziget Festival in Budapest alongside Pink and the Chainsmokers, he plans to make his first official music video and continue hitting the road. "In the future, I want to be one of those people where other artists might say, 'I got to headline with Jaimie Wilson.' "

Pretty Hurts While he has received an outpouring of support about his trans identity, there are plenty of detractors both online and off. "I had people tell me I can't be transgender because I was such a pretty girl or because I didn't show the signs," he said. "I want to show other people out there that despite what you look like or how people view you, you can do whatever you want."

Jackie Shane, a Transgender Soul Pioneer, Re-emerges After Four Decades

BY REGGIE UGWU | OCT. 15, 2017

IN AUGUST 2016, Douglas Mcgowan arrived at a modest brick house near central Nashville with a contract and the faint hope of a face-to-face meeting with the home's mysterious occupant.

Mr. Mcgowan, a scout for the archival record label the Numero Group, was looking for Jackie Shane, a venerated but misunderstood soul singer who had not been seen in public in nearly five decades. He had obtained Ms. Shane's phone number three years earlier through a friend of hers, and the pair had developed what felt like a genuine long distance friendship — he engaged her on current affairs over lengthy, discursive phone calls and steered clear of prying personal questions; she teased him with a nickname, "Hot lips," and told him he sounded short.

At Ms. Shane's house in Nashville, Mr. Mcgowan had envisioned a climactic rendezvous. But it never happened.

"I'm not ready," Mr. Mcgowan said Ms. Shane called out from the other side of a wall. After two hours of debating in the summer heat, he finally gave up, leaving the contract — an agreement for Ms. Shane to work with the Numero Group to reissue her catalog — on her front doorstep.

To Mr. Mcgowan's relief, she signed it.

The reissue, a two-disc boxed set with extensive liner notes called "Any Other Way," comes out Oct. 20. It is the first comprehensive collection of Ms. Shane's music, which electrified primarily Canadian audiences throughout the 1960s. In 1963, the title track — a buttery William Bell cover — was a local hit on Toronto radio and peaked at No. 2 on the singles chart there, ahead of Skeeter Davis's "The End of the World" and below the Chiffons' "He's So Fine."

Ms. Shane walked away from her career without explanation in 1971. In the intervening decades, she has become an internet curiosity and minor cult heroine among soul music aficionados who have spun crackpot theories as to her whereabouts and well-being.

Over two telephone calls this fall, Ms. Shane, who is now 77, spoke to The New York Times for her first-ever extensive interviews with the press, and first public remarks of any kind since she disappeared 46 years ago.

She was eager to break her silence.

"I told Sam and Doug: If you want me to be phony, you've got the wrong person," Ms. Shane said, referring to her publicist and Mr. Mcgowan.

She was born in Nashville in 1940, black and transgender at a time when either meant a life of constriction and compromise. Before she ever set foot on a stage, Ms. Shane's existence was itself a tightrope walk, pitched between third rails in the Jim Crow South.

Though she said she self-identified as a woman in a man's body by the time she was 13, Ms. Shane occasionally described herself to peers as gay — several decades before the movement for transgender rights altered the discourse around gender and sexuality. Throughout her career, she was referred to publicly as a man.

"I was just being me," she said. "I never tried to explain myself to anyone — they never explained themselves to me."

Around 1959, she emigrated to Toronto, where she wore wigs and makeup onstage and off — typically paired with fur, silk or sequins. In front of rapt nightclub audiences, when she sang with husky, quavering verve, or turned interstitial monologues into febrile, secular sermons, she was exhibiting a kind of radical transparency.

Ms. Shane's memorable rendition of "Any Other Way" contains a line — "Tell her that I'm happy, tell her that I'm gay" — that she imbued with subversive subtext.

"You know, you're supposed to live," she says in a monologue from the live version included on the boxed set, outlining her own liberation theology. "As long as you don't force your will and your way on others, forget 'em, baby, you don't need 'em."

Before she left the grid in 1971, Ms. Shane studied under Little Richard and the Upsetters, and shared stages with Etta James, Jackie Wilson and the Impressions, among other R&B and soul icons. But she never recorded a studio album, in part because of the fledgling state of Canada's music industry at the time and her own distrust of record labels. In the years after she stopped performing, Ms. Shane's star, like that of so many almost-famous performers dotting the universe of postwar popular music, quietly dimmed.

Ms. Shane said she'd spent the better part of the last five decades in Los Angeles, where she first moved to be with her mother, Jessie Shane. Ms. Shane's stepfather died in 1963, and the singer said she felt guilty pursuing a career thousands of miles away while her mother lived alone. So she left it behind, and cared for her mother until her death in 1997.

In Nashville, Ms. Shane has sought a clean break from her past. She said she moved back eight or nine years ago and now lives alone.

She is reclusive and ventures outside only rarely — once a month for supplies (including pet food: her black-and-gold cat is named Sweetie), or for the occasional walk. She declined to say how she's supported herself, but said she's never had a job other than music.

When Ms. Shane does leave the house, she dresses in a hat and sunglasses out of fear of being recognized. She estimates that her neighbors have spotted her only "three or four" times in the near decade since she moved in.

"I don't mingle," she said, because "down South, gossiping and meddling is like breathing."

She was at times unapologetically misanthropic, tracing her distrust of others to her upbringing in Nashville. As a child, Ms. Shane turned heads by speaking and dressing in an openly feminine manner from an early age. She disarmed busybodies and browbeaters with preternatural self-confidence and an innate survival instinct that could turn ferocious.

For example, she recalled a schoolyard bully who made the mistake of striking her with a stone in the fourth grade. "He wanted to torment me and I would never allow that," Ms. Shane said, still defiant. She used a jump rope to thrash him — and then, in a fight-or-flight fury, turned the whip on a teacher who attempted to intervene.

Not all of her antagonists were as conventional. Ms. Shane said she had twice escaped inappropriate touching from older men who were friends of her family, beginning when she was as young as five. The experiences shaded her worldview.

Recent advances in gay and transgender rights have done little to brighten it. Asked for her thoughts on the Supreme Court's 2015 decision upholding gay marriage, Ms. Shane expressed limited enthusiasm. "We should have been able to do it from the beginning," she said. "We've had to fight for everything that should have already been on the table."

Today, her domestic life is both extraordinary and familiar. Ms. Shane has never learned to cook ("I'm a terror in the kitchen, honey — I could set water on fire") and has food catered four to five times per week (when craving strikes, she orders from Domino's). She says she's accumulated an extensive library of movies and TV shows, and enjoys watching old Hollywood films with stars like Peter Lorre, Humphrey Bogart, Bette Davis and Joan Crawford.

Lately, though, she's been binge-watching the NBC fantasy drama "Grimm," about a homicide detective who discovers a hidden world of mythological creatures.

"Every culture has some kind of boogeyman," she said.

After the release of Ms. Shane's anthology, Mr. Mcgowan is hopeful that renewed interest will prompt her to return to public life, and — in a perfect world — the stage. Ms. Shane made no such promises in her interviews. But, she said, a recent glance at the popular music landscape has at least stirred the thought.

"I'm going to have to school these people again," she said.

CHAPTER 3

Television

In 2014, Jill Soloway's "Transparent" premiered on Amazon. The show followed the Pfefferman family as the family patriarch, Mort, transitions to become Maura. This show followed Netflix's "Orange Is the New Black," the television show set in a women's prison, that broke ground by featuring Laverne Cox as a transgender inmate named Sophia. Together, these shows made an important statement about the importance of transgender stories in the entertainment industry: they are here to stay.

In Their Own Terms: The Growing Transgender Presence in Pop Culture

BY JACOB BERNSTEIN | MARCH 12, 2014

THE FIRST TIME Rhys Ernst saw Zackary Drucker was in 2005 at a bar in the East Village.

At the time, both were aspiring artists. Rhys had recently graduated from Hampshire College and was working for MTV networks. Zackary had graduated from the School of Visual Arts and was appearing on a reality TV show called "Artstar," hosted by Jeffrey Deitch.

But there was one clear impediment to romance: Rhys had never dated a man, and Zackary had never dated a woman.

"I remember thinking," Rhys said, "if I ever dated a boy, that's the type of boy I'd date."

Today, that consideration is not an issue. Over the last five years, Zackary has transitioned from male to female, Rhys from female to male.

And in "Relationship," a photo exhibition currently on view at the Whitney Biennial, the two have chronicled that process and the evolution of their own love affair. (In a recent preview of the Biennial, Holland Cotter of The New York Times wrote that the Ernst/Drucker photographs "put queer consciousness on the front burner.")

That a show by two transgender artists should be so prominently featured at the 2014 Biennial should come as a surprise to no one. It is just more evidence of the increasing presence of trans people at the center of popular culture.

In their spring advertising campaigns, the luxury retailer Barneys New York and the award-winning jewelry designer Alexis Bittar feature transgender models. In February, a memoir by Janet Mock, a former editor at People magazine, which drew heavily on her transition from male to female, made the New York Times best-seller list. Laverne Cox has become a breakout star on Netflix's hit show "Orange Is the New Black," playing a sympathetic character who winds up in prison after using stolen credit cards to pay for her gender reassignment surgery. And Carmen Carrera, a transgender showgirl who first achieved demi-fame as a contestant on the reality television program "RuPaul's Drag Race," has become an in-demand fashion model and muse for the photographer Steven Meisel.

Here are their stories.

LAVERNE COX

Laverne Cox grew up in Mobile, Ala., with her identical twin brother and her mother, a single parent who worked two to three jobs at a time to make ends meet.

She enrolled at Marymount Manhattan College in New York in the late '90s, where by day she majored in dance, took her first acting classes and became immersed in gender studies.

By night, Ms. Cox was a presence on the downtown club scene, hanging out at Flamingo East in the East Village and performing operatic versions of heavy metal songs at Squeeze Box, a Friday night party at Don Hill's. (Among the songs she sang were Iron Maiden's "Be Quick or Be Dead" and Pantera's "Mouth for War.")

At the time, Ms. Cox said, she was in a "gender nonconforming space," no longer living as a man, but still struggling with her own "internalized transphobia" as well as a desire to "be myself and not embody some stereotype of womanhood."

"It was a mess," she said.

After completing her transition, she was cast in 2008 on the VH1 reality show "I Want to Work for Diddy." (Ms. Cox made it halfway through the competition.) Last year, she got her big break with a role on "Orange Is the New Black" on Netflix.

On the show, the major characters appear in prison and then in flashback sequences that show how they got there. So Ms. Cox's twin, a musician who lives in Brooklyn, played her character pretransition.

Ms. Cox has spoken at colleges about the transgender experience. She's also done one now-famous chat on a daytime talk show, where she appeared with Carmen Carrera and gently chastised the host, Katie Couric, for being too focused on questions about genital surgery, which not every transgender person undergoes. After Ms. Couric said to Ms. Carrera, "Your private parts are different now, aren't they," Ms. Cox argued that focusing on this objectifies trans people and prevents a more meaningful discussion from taking place.

"Someone called me a man in the airport today," Ms. Cox said in an interview this week. "Just because there's a few trans folks having lovely careers and having moments of visibility does not mean that a lot of trans folks lives are not in peril. We need to remember those folks who are struggling, particularly trans women of color who are on the margins."

JANET MOCK

Some success stories are neat. Others, like Janet Mock's, less so. She grew up in Hawaii with a mother who had her first child at 16 and a father who battled drug addiction and had numerous children with

Janet Mock, whose forthcoming book is titled "Surpassing Certainty: What My 20s Taught Me."

other women. (One year, Ms. Mock said, her father "had a baby in January, February and April.")

Then, in middle school, Ms. Mock met a transgender girl named Wendi, and at 12 or 13, she began applying lip gloss, wearing makeup and tweezing her eyebrows. At 15, she started hormones.

She was an honor student in high school while she worked as a prostitute on Merchant Street in Honolulu, which is how she saved the money to travel to Thailand and pay for gender reassignment surgery.

After graduating from the University of Hawaii in 2005, Ms. Mock became an editor at People.com, then came out as transgender in a 2011 Marie Claire profile.

This winter, Atria Books (a division of Simon and Schuster) published her memoir, "Redefining Realness," in which she quotes Audre Lorde, James Baldwin and Maya Angelou but wrote that Beyoncé was most responsible for "shifting" how she viewed herself as a woman of color.

"Everyone celebrated her because she was the girl of the moment," said Ms. Mock, 31, who has frizzy, Afro-ish hair with blond highlights, and, on the day I met her, looked effortlessly fashionable in a pair of black Theory jeans and a denim shirt with the sleeves rolled up, showing off her gold-colored infinity bangles. On her arm was a tan leather 3.1 Phillip Lim bag, which she said was a gift to herself after her book became a best seller.

Like Ms. Cox and Ms. Carrera, she has been somewhat offended by the tone of some of her television interviews. Last month, Ms. Mock went on Piers Morgan's CNN show (it has since been canceled), where the host all but began the interview by saying how "amazing" it was that this attractive woman had once been biologically male.

"Had I not known your life story, I would have absolutely no clue," he said, as the scrawl at the bottom of the bottom of the screen read "Born a boy."

Ms. Mock pounced on Twitter, and Slate ran a withering piece on Mr. Morgan's performance that evening, chastising him for being "obsessed with appearances" and accusing the show of promoting the segment in a "sensational and ignorant way."

Nevertheless, the interest in Ms. Mock's book and its subsequent sales is an indication that something is changing dramatically. And, no doubt, she appreciates having a platform now.

As a child, she said: "All I knew was gay. All I knew was RuPaul."

VALENTIJN DE HINGH

A Dutch camera crew followed Valentijn de Hingh around for the bulk of her childhood, chronicling her journey from male to female. By the end of high school, she was walking in runway shows for Comme des Garçons and Maison Martin Margiela. In 2012, she gave a talk at a TEDx event in Amsterdam titled "Why Did I Choose?" This year, she is appearing in the Barneys campaign alongside 16 other transgender models.

Having understanding parents helped, she said.

They first read about transgender children in a magazine when Ms. de Hingh was 5 and took her to a hospital in the Netherlands with a program for gender-variant children.

"My parents were looking for answers, and they found it there," she said.

Schoolmates, she said, were largely accepting, though she did experience some taunting. Being openly transgender but preoperative made dating hard, something she struggles with, even after gender reassignment surgery.

"I still have a hard time with dating," said Ms. de Hingh, 23. "I have some figuring out to do."

RHYS ERNST AND ZACKARY DRUCKER

Many of the photographs in Zackary Drucker and Rhys Ernst's show at the Whitney capture them in scenarios most couples can relate to: celebrating anniversaries, lounging around the house while one fights off a cold, sitting poolside on a sunny day.

Others depict circumstances that are perhaps unique to a transgender couple, such as an image of Mr. Ernst's and Ms. Drucker's bandage-covered backsides shortly after taking hormone shots.

According to Ms. Drucker, the exhibition has a couple of aims. One is to show that all relationships are in some way banal. Another, she said, is about "learning to love ourselves and deflect the distortions" that prevent people from doing that.

There weren't a lot of transgender role models for Ms. Drucker and Mr. Ernst growing up. But their parents were progressive and supported their children's gender nonconformity.

In high school, they both became familiar with the writings of Kate Bornstein, a queer theorist whose books "Gender Outlaw: On Men, Women and the Rest of Us," and "My Gender Workbook: How to Become a Real Man, a Real Woman, the Real You, or Something Else Entirely" outlined a way of living that did not ascribe to traditional gender conventions.

"I don't call myself a woman, and I know I'm not a man," Ms. Bornstein once said.

Today, the couple lives in Los Angeles and has been consulting on the pilot of a television show for Amazon called "Transparent." It stars Jeffrey Tambor of "Arrested Development" as an aging man who is beginning a gender transition. (It was picked up on Tuesday.)

They are also part of a wide circle of "gender queer" and transgender creative types that includes Wu Tsang (a filmmaker and visual artist who identifies as "transfeminine" and "transguy") and Amos Mac, a photographer and editor who runs Originalplumbing, a magazine and website, that are devoted to hipsterish transgender types.

This pretty much describes Ms. Drucker, 30, who has a penchant for tight leggings, vintage Yves Saint Laurent heels and Grecian tops — and yet has no plans to have gender reassignment surgery, a topic she discusses pretty openly.

The same goes for Mr. Ernst, 31, who sports a light goatee and on Friday was wearing a button-down shirt with high tops and charcoal pants.

Ultimately, Ms. Drucker said, she'd like to get to a point where we "surpass" the binaries of gender altogether.

"That would be the greatest transition of all," she said.

Broadening a Transgender Tale That Has Only Just Begun

BY ERIK PIEPENBURG | JUNE 19, 2015

"WHAT A DIFFERENCE it makes when an actual trans person plays the role."

That was Laverne Cox's reflection in 2011 on how, after years of intermittent visibility, transgender actors like herself were being cast more frequently in films and on television as honest-to-goodness transgender characters. (Mostly women.) Four years later, Ms. Cox has an Emmy Award nomination for her role in the Netflix series "Orange Is the New Black," now in its third season on Netflix, and will be seen this summer as an old friend of Lily Tomlin's in the film "Grandma." She is leveraging her success to redefine, physically and culturally, what it means to be an actress.

But what about other transgender performers? Has Ms. Cox's breakout widened their chances in the audition room or inaugurated a new wave of transgender characters? Conversations with several transgender actors working in film and on television suggest that Ms. Cox's rise to stardom has rewritten the rules.

"We have come a long way, especially in the past two years or so since 'Orange' hit," said Trace Lysette, who plays a trans yoga instructor on the Amazon series "Transparent." "Laverne is the one who really kicked the door open and let people on to the fact that we can have a real story line and really be human."

The new crop of transgender talent includes many actors making their debuts, including Mya Taylor, a star of "Tangerine," a hit at the Sundance Film Festival scheduled to reach theaters next month, and Michelle Hendley, who as the star of the recent coming-of-age film "Boy Meets Girl" has a bold nude scene. Others, like Alexandra Billings, who plays a worldly confidante to Jeffrey Tambor's character, a transgender parent of three in "Transparent," are reaching wider audiences after years of under-the-radar roles.

Actress Laverne Cox poses for a portrait in The New York Times building prior to an interview in 2015.

Brad Calcaterra, a New York acting teacher who counts Ms. Cox among his students, said the number of transgender actors in his classes had exploded. "Art doesn't have gender," he said.

Tom Phelan, who plays a transgender teenager on the ABC Family show "The Fosters," said that as more young trans people like himself have joined the national acting pool, there has been an increase in rich roles that ask actors to dig deep emotionally.

He recalls taping a scene set at a beach that required him to remove his shirt. "The camera sees my scars, which I think is cool," he said. "If I were a young trans man living somewhere where there is little information, that would be amazing to see on television."

Recently these actors spoke about the newly opened doors they've walked through and the challenges to come. Here are excerpts from those conversations.

Q. *How would you describe the environment for transgender actors?*

Tom Phelan We are in a better place than ever before. They are not only drawing from the same two people. But it's still slim pickings.

Alexandra Billings There are more opportunities, but look carefully. They're very specific. We're either in the hospital or visiting someone in the hospital or in jail or some kind of cage. God forbid you put us in charge of children or in the corporate world, where we have power. We're having specific conversations, but it's difficult to say it's getting better.

Trace Lysette When we get to a point when trans folks are included in the creative process, the narrative will be much more authentic. Trans actors playing trans roles is a key part of that. But some of the trans talent is not even making it into the audition room, let's be honest.

Q. *Have you experienced discrimination on the set?*

Laverne Cox I've had moments when I've been misgendered by folks on set, where someone used the wrong pronoun. Earlier in my career, I might have taken that personally and lost focus. But I've learned that when those moments happen, if it won't take me out of the work, I will gently correct them. If it will take me out of what I'm there to do, then I go on with the work. At the end of the day, what is on screen is what matters most.

Lysette Nothing too negative, just educational moments about certain terms that people may not know. You wish that everyone knew what cisgender meant. Everyone has access to Google. You can find out what's appropriate to ask a trans person.

Mya Taylor Our crew was very familiar with trans people. They were very cautious that they could say certain things. Everybody was very respectful.

Michelle Hendley In my daily life, I deal with that. It's important to understand where people are coming from. Are they trying to hurt your feelings? Or do they just not understand? I'm open to educating people.

Q. *There has been a push on shows like "Modern Family" to make gay people seem just like everyone else. But there are big differences between the gay and straight worlds. Do you think roles that treat transgender characters as next-door-neighbor types might be erasing what makes transgender people unique?*

Cox Me embracing my trans identity but also my identity as a black woman from a working-class background from the South, all of these things make me special. I'm not interested in erasing. In some ways trans people are like everybody else, and in some ways we are not. When we get specific in the storytelling, that's when the universality happens.

Billings People say to me: "I don't see color. I have black friends, but they are just like me." I think to myself, if you don't see an African-American human being standing in front of you, you're either a liar or need medication. Our transgender life is rooted in history. You can go back to the Greeks and see us. When I say we are your neighbors, we are, but we will not be erased. We will be thought of. In order to do that, you have to know that I am transgender. This is a tricky conversation in this community.

Phelan I would love where someone happens to be trans, but other than that it was like one character attribute of a very well-rounded person. We are moving toward that. I know that for the rest of the world, you've got to ease them into it, as much as you don't want to. You have to provide them with a very bland version of this thing to be a gateway into it, and then as you move along you can have more in-depth story lines.

Q. *What transgender stories aren't we seeing on film and TV?*

Cox The challenges for trans women who date straight identified men, those stories are really not told. I think the men who date trans women are even more stigmatized than trans women are. And until recently, most trans stories out there were focused on transition and surgery and bodies. We are so much more than that.

Taylor I think one of the biggest things is growing up, being a little kid, what goes on in a household. I was a boy, and the household I lived in wasn't as accepting, so I had to hide everything. I would wear makeup, and my parents would go into my room and throw it in the trash. There are so many stories.

Lysette If you can go through everyday life, get on the subway and make it to work without an incident or someone shouting, "That's a man!," you're blending with heteronormative folks, and that's a really interesting story that hasn't been told yet. As much of a privilege as it is to pass, it's painful. You have to compartmentalize your life. That's awkward. Dating can be horrible. That's a really deep story that hasn't been told. Trans male stories definitely need to be told.

Hendley Ten or 15 years ago, we thought "Will & Grace" had normalized the gay community for America. I'm hoping we can get to that point where we will have those characters, but the central point is not just that they are transgender. They will just be your best friend. That's the ultimate goal.

Billings I really would love to see some transgender people in something light and silly. Terrible things are always happening to us, which is true, and I understand that. But I would love to see something like "I Love Lucy." We're just as funny and light as we are dark. If you've got a pie, throw it in my face.

Q. *What's your advice for young transgender people interested in pursuing an acting career?*

Cox There are all kinds of aesthetic realities about the business that can be frustrating for people who identify on different places on the transgender spectrum. Everyone who is transgender doesn't necessarily transition from male to female or female to male. Some people identify as bigender or agender or genderqueer. That will affect your ability to work. At the end of the day, it's about creating your own opportunities when you can.

Phelan It's the same I'd give to any actor. Disappointment is the worst thing to live with, but sometimes you've got to live with it. Don't be ashamed of the person you are. Don't feel you have to change anything about yourself to fit what other people want. Trying to be the leading man is probably something you aren't if you are trans, and that's O.K.

Laverne Cox: 'Blending In Was Never an Option'

BY ERIC SPITZNAGEL | MAY 29, 2014

THE ACTRESS TALKS to Eric Spitznagel about growing up in the South, the difficulties of writing a memoir and the fortuitous casting decision that landed her on "Orange Is the New Black."

Q. *You play a transgender character, Sophia, on "Orange Is the New Black." Were they specifically looking for a transgender person to play the role?*

A. I've heard that they were looking for someone trans. Jenji Kohan [the show's creator] says they had a joke in the writers' room that they ideally wanted to hire a trans woman who had an identical twin brother.

Q. *That's true for you. On the show, he plays your character in pretransition flashbacks.*

A. That is true. It was a joke, but you just have to put it out into the universe, and it happens.

Q. *What did he think of all this?*

A. To be perfectly honest, he was like, How much does it pay? He's a musician, and he's struggling financially, so it was about the money for him.

Q. *Your character was married with a kid before she made her transition, which, it seems, she paid for by committing credit-card fraud. You discovered your gender identity a little earlier in life, right?*

A. Absolutely. I don't have children, and I don't want children. I've never dated a woman ever. But I think there's something in Sophia that we all can relate to as human beings, about not wanting to disappoint family. Her shame about the things she's done really made me connect to her.

Q. *Were your parents immediately accepting of your identity?*

A. What took time for my mom was getting the pronouns right and calling me by a different name. Laverne was my middle name before I transitioned. But I was an adult when I told her. It was her decision whether she wanted to accept me or not, and she did. I'm writing a book now, so I interviewed my mom about what she knew when I was young, and she was in crazy denial.

Q. *Was it hard to objectively report on your own life?*

A. It's funny, my mother and I remember things completely differently. In certain instances, I'll say my mother remembers it this way — but this is my book. What's difficult is remembering details; it's intensely painful. I'll write for a couple of hours and then start crying for like half an hour.

Q. *You grew up in Alabama, and you were very involved in your church. That doesn't strike me as an environment open to the concept of gender fluidity.*

A. It does seem there's a "don't ask, don't tell" kind of policy in my church. There were gay men in my church who we all knew were gay. But no one talked about it. I've talked to other black folks in the South, and there's a lot of those sort of policies.

Q. *What about at school?*

A. One teacher called my mother and said I'd end up in New Orleans wearing a dress if she didn't get me therapy.

Q. *Sophia is the first transgender person a lot of audiences will be exposed to, and she's in prison. Do you worry that's sending the wrong message?*

A. I think our show really makes it explicit that just because someone is incarcerated does not mean they are no longer a human being. We can't talk about America without talking about this. We incarcerate more people than anybody else in the world. I'm not interested in this false dichotomy around positive versus negative representation. It does not allow for the complexity and the nuance and the full humanity of character.

Q. *You've said that Sophia has helped people come out.*

A. Earlier this year, a woman in Canada was in tears as she met me. She said that watching the show allowed her to be able to have a conversation with her wife about her desire to transition. She's almost done now, and she's still in the relationship.

Q. *Is it a burden to be known as a transgender actress — not just an actress?*

A. Yeah, but at the same time I think it's important to empower being trans. Most of the narrative around trans identity has been about transitioning. You blend in, and that is the goal, but blending in was never an option for me. Some people are going to know that we're trans. There's nothing wrong with that.

Q. *Will we live to see a day when there's a transgender crime-scene investigator on a "C.S.I." spinoff?*

A. This is my dream! This is my dream! I actually believe it is possible.

For Laverne Cox, Life Is a Blur, and So Is New York

BY LEAH ROZEN | OCT. 13, 2016

LAVERNE COX was on the 102nd floor of One World Trade Center, gazing north through the floor-to-ceiling windows. Manhattan's skyscrapers glinted in the midday sunlight.

"I've been missing New York so much," she said, reaching out as if to embrace the city. "I'm scared of heights, but oh, my God, to get back and to get to see this. It's like ummmm-mmhhh!"

She waved to the spire of the Empire State Building, saying that it's near her current apartment, a rent-stabilized place she moved into while still a struggling actress. "I ain't going nowhere," she vowed in true New Yorker style.

This striking Emmy-nominated transgender actress and activist,

The actress Laverne Cox at One World Observatory. "I've been missing New York so much," she said.

best known for her role as Sophia, a transgender inmate on "Orange Is the New Black" on Netflix, was back in the city for a quickie visit in late August.

She was squeezing in a tour of the One World Observatory — she had been invited for a private viewing — and lunch before flying back to Los Angeles later that day. She's living there temporarily while filming "Doubt," a new legal drama in which she stars as a crusading, Yale-educated, transgender lawyer. It's scheduled to begin on CBS in early 2017.

Ms. Cox, dressed in a slinky black Marciano dress and 6 feet 3 inches in her four-inch Louboutins, was unsure of her flight time, though she knew a car was coming at 4:30 p.m. to deliver her to the airport.

Her life has been a busy blur since her success on "Orange" in 2013, and she's still on the show. There was that cover of Time magazine in 2014, there is "Doubt," and she will be rocking fishnet stockings and a spangled red corset as Dr. Frank-N-Furter in a new version of "The Rocky Horror Picture Show," the 1975 cult movie musical, to be broadcast on Fox on Oct. 20.

"Rocky" showcases her four-octave singing range — "I can sing baritone and soprano" — and her dancing. Ms. Cox earned a bachelor of fine arts in dance from Marymount Manhattan College but said she was much younger then: "I can still do a split, but these days I have to stretch before I do it."

Friendly and funny, Ms. Cox, raised in Mobile, Ala., answers any and all questions — well, almost all. "Age and weight we don't do," she said, explaining that being black and transgender puts enough hurdles in her career path. She believes revealing her age would only add another.

"I'm living this life that is the life I've dreamed of my whole life and that most people don't get to live," Ms. Cox said. "Now this is very recent and, God willing, I'll be able to keep it going."

From 102 stories up, Ms. Cox spotted the Statue of Liberty. She filmed it on her phone while reciting from the poem "The New Colossus"

"I'm scared of heights, but oh, my God, to get back and to get to see this," Ms. Cox said of the views from One World Trade Center. "It's like ummmm-mmhhh!"

by Emma Lazarus in a dramatic tone, "Give me your tired, your poor, your huddled masses yearning to breathe free." She'd be posting that on Snapchat, she said, adding, "I'm such a dork."

After the tour, Ms. Cox shed her heels for flats ("They're from Amazon.com") and walked a block to Blue Smoke, a Danny Meyer-owned restaurant. Passers-by did double takes, and a few called out greetings, to which Ms. Cox gave a friendly nod.

The restaurant's Southern-fried chicken had her salivating, but instead she ordered deviled eggs ("That's mostly protein"), hush puppies, a shrimp sandwich and an unsweetened iced tea. "When I was under 21, I could eat whatever I wanted and not gain a pound," she said. "After transitioning, when I stopped producing testosterone, I just filled out, and I kept filling."

Over lunch, she whipped through topics.

Yes, she'll be voting for Hillary Clinton in the election and considers much of Donald J. Trump's rhetoric racist. "It's not a dog whistle; it's a bark," she said. "And I think Republicans are trying to use trans as a wedge issue, the same way they used gay marriage in the last election."

Yes, her post-"Orange" celebrity has improved her love life. "The trans thing — fame mitigates that for a lot of the men," she said. "It makes them more willing and open to dating me than they might have been before." (She currently has a steady beau.)

The waitress brought a dessert menu, but Ms. Cox waved it away. Not without some reluctance, it seemed.

"If you could eat as much ice cream as you want and not get fat, and not get high cholesterol and diabetes, I would never have sex again," she said. "I would just curl up every night with a pint of Ben & Jerry's Chocolate Chip Cookie Dough ice cream, and I would be good."

How Two Producers of 'Transparent' Made Their Own Trans Lives More Visible

BY EMILY BOBROW | SEPT. 13, 2016

ON A HOT NIGHT IN JULY at Skylight Books in Los Angeles, Zackary Drucker and Rhys Ernst perched on stools to discuss their new book of photographs, "Relationship." It is by far the most personal of the many projects they have worked on together. The photographs chronicle their six-year romance, which ended soon after many of these images were shown at the Whitney Biennial in 2014.

Drucker and Ernst, who are perhaps better known as producers of the Emmy-winning Amazon series "Transparent," speak regularly about their work. But Drucker is plainly more at ease in the spotlight. She is tall and blond, with eyes as blue as swimming pools. That night she wore a white shift and high-heeled sling-backs, and she kept the microphone in its stand so she could gesture with her hands. The images, she told the audience, were meant as a private visual diary. "There was never an intent to show the photographs, even though we are both art-makers."

They are both 33 and around the same height, but Ernst appears slighter. Wearing light brown pants, bright white Reeboks and a dia-mond stud in his right ear, he explained that he and Drucker have backgrounds in "auto-ethnography," which he defined as "the prac-tice of creating self-reflexive work, or work that reflected my com-munity." This, he said, was a guiding impulse for the photographs in "Relationship."

Anyone familiar with the rush of young love will recognize its hall-marks in these photos: all smoldering looks, parted lips and bare limbs on rumpled sheets. Drucker and Ernst have an easy sexual charisma, but that's not what makes this series novel, even daring. During the years they were together, from 2008 to 2014, Drucker was in the process of transitioning from male to female, and Ernst from female to male. They met soon after they each began taking hormones, so the photographs also capture what Ernst has described as "the unflattering throes of yet another puberty." In calling this series "Relationship," Drucker and Ernst are describing not only their partnership but also their relationship with themselves and their genders, their choices and their bodies.

Though Drucker and Ernst are no longer a couple, they chose to publish these photographs anyway, because even as transgender stories are becoming more mainstream, there are few public examples of trans people leading ordinary lives, filled with love and lazy mornings. There are even fewer cases, as Drucker and Ernst emphasized that night in July, of trans people taking control over how they are represented.

On "Transparent," whose third season begins this month, their goal has been to ensure not just that trans people are depicted accurately on screen, but also that they are working behind the scenes — as writers, directors and personal assistants. Except for the character of Maura, a father who comes out to his family as trans, played by Jeffrey Tambor, every trans role on the show is filled by a trans person. The desire to see more transgender people in front of and behind the camera also informs much of Drucker's and Ernst's work as artists. Drucker is often the star of her own experimental videos and performances, which challenge conventional views of sex and gender. Her work has been shown at MoMA's PS1, the Museum of Contemporary Art in Chicago and SFMoMA. Ernst's narrative filmmaking tends to feature trans actors and documentary subjects and travel the film-festival circuit. He is at work on his first full-length feature, which he describes as a "middle-aged trans-guy buddy-movie comedy."

"I remember when we were installing the photographs at the Whitney, someone asked us: 'Oh, this is great. Who was the photographer?'" Ernst told the bookstore crowd. "They assumed we were just the subjects, which is of course the history of this kind of work. But this is what I hope changes going forward. It's the work we're doing in television. It's the work we're doing in filmmaking. It's the work we're doing in photography. It's making trans people the author, rather than just the subject. That's really the key."

Pop-cultural representations of trans people have historically reduced them to objects of pity or scorn. "Over and over again, somebody is crying in the mirror, taking off their wig," Ernst said over dinner at a gastropub near the Silver Lake home he shares with his partner, Patrick Staff, an artist. "There are these fixations that cisgender people get that are not the way our lives are being lived at all." (To be "cis-gender" is to identify as the gender you are assigned at birth; i.e., not trans.) A prime example, he said, is "Dallas Buyers Club," a critically acclaimed film that earned Jared Leto an Oscar in 2014 for his supporting role as Rayon, an H.I.V.-positive trans woman. "She was a throwaway character," Ernst griped, "a drug addict who was there to make the protagonist learn about himself, and she was named after a synthetic fabric. That's not a real person."

In the two years since, there has been a marked political and cultural shift, and a growing public fascination with trans people. For Drucker and Ernst, whose work has always been about making the trans experience more visible, this has meant a much bigger audience. "There needs to be a little demystifying about trans existence," Ernst said. "That's why people have so many burning questions about it all."

Soon after their photographs were installed at the Whitney, they began working on the first season of "Transparent" with Jill Soloway, the show's creator. Soloway met Ernst when they each had a short film screening at the Sundance Film Festival in 2012. Soloway's father had just come out as trans, and she found herself opening up to Ernst about what she was going through. They kept in touch. After Soloway finished writing the "Transparent" pilot, she reached out to Ernst and Drucker, knowing that she needed trans people involved from the start. "Everyone knows and loves them," she told me in her office on the Paramount lot. "They're the homecoming king and queen of the trans movement."

Drucker and Ernst say the show has been able to "undo a lot of damage" when it comes to popular portrayals of trans people. Maura is not a sad loner whose every act and thought is about transitioning. Rather, she is the parent of a flawed but loving family in which everyone seems uncomfortable in their skin. Initially hired as consultants to prevent the show from trafficking in trans stereotypes, Drucker and Ernst were swiftly promoted to producers. They now offer notes on scripts, watch rough cuts of episodes and work closely with the writers and actors to make the trans performances as authentic as possible. Drucker helps Tambor understand how Maura feels about herself and her body, and she tweaks his mannerisms onscreen, regularly nudging him to close his legs, for example. Ernst directs the opening credits. Both also lead what they call "Trans 101" for everyone involved with the show, from Amazon executives to truck drivers, in which they explain the etiquette of working with trans colleagues. They stress that it is best to ask what pronoun people prefer. They advise against inquiring about the genitals or birth names of trans people, or referring to them as "trannies" or "she-males." "People are afraid of saying the wrong thing, so they don't have the conversation," Drucker says. "But I think there's no undignified questions, only undignified answers."

For many of the show's trans performers and crew members, all of this has been life-changing. "'Transparent' was my coming-out party," Trace Lysette said at the show's panel at Outfest, the L.G.B.T. film festival in Los Angeles, in July. Like many trans women, Lysette struggled for years to find employment, making money by stripping and sex work before she landed a recurring role as Shea, a friend of Maura's. "It's allowed me to get up off the pole and have a career that I never thought would really happen," she said. Silas Howard, the show's first trans director, says the call from Soloway was like getting "a golden ticket." Tambor has begun teaching acting classes for trans people in Los Angeles.

Drian Juarez, the program manager of the Transgender Economic Empowerment Project, a Los Angeles nonprofit group, told me that the show's success has inspired other companies, including NBC and Ryan Seacrest Productions, to ask her for leads on transgender talent for trans-related stories. Given that trans people are twice as likely to be unemployed as the general population (four times as likely if they are not white), these industry jobs are a big deal. Drucker and Ernst also persuaded Amazon to sponsor the Trans Pride festival in Los Angeles.

"I've just never seen any production like the familial, politicized, life-changing, worldview-changing empathy machine that is 'Transparent,'" Ernst told me. The show, he conceded, doesn't exactly represent a new norm in the industry, but he and Drucker hope that the many trans people involved in its production are gaining the tools necessary to make their own shows. "It's certainly the beginning of something new," Drucker says.

For the moment, working on "Transparent" has turned Drucker and Ernst into trans spokespeople in Hollywood. Drucker was among the trans women hired to help Caitlyn Jenner navigate her new trans life on the two-season E! Network series "I Am Cait." Focus Features asked Ernst to be a consultant on "The Danish Girl," a 2015 biopic about Lili Elbe, one of the first people to undergo gender-reassignment surgery. Ernst was wary, as the film was already underway with a cis-gender writer, director and star. Yet he found the studio receptive to his many recommendations, including his request that Focus "give back to the trans community in tangible ways." The studio created a $10,000 scholarship for trans filmmakers and helped fund a web series of documentary shorts about trans pioneers called "We've Been Around," directed by Ernst, which had its premiere online in March. "Being trans right now necessitates this multihyphenate way of being," Drucker says.

When Drucker and Ernst were growing up in the 1990s, mass media presented trans people mainly on talk shows like "Jerry Springer," which tended to sensationalize with big reveals like "My Boyfriend Is a Girl!" and "Guess What ... I'm a Man!" "You knew you didn't want to be that, but at least there was something to point to," Drucker said. We were eating homemade tabbouleh at her house in Cypress Park, which she shares with her boyfriend of nearly two years, Jerid Bartow, an urban designer.

Finding models for how to live, or even a language to describe their feelings, was difficult for Drucker and Ernst. After Drucker discovered that she desired boys and Ernst that he liked girls (at least initially), they didn't feel right calling themselves gay or lesbian because it didn't feel as if they were attracted to the same sex. They were both relieved as teenagers to discover the term "queer," which is elastic enough to elide standard definitions of sexual orientation and gender.

Each was raised in a supportive home by compassionate parents — a rare privilege, they acknowledge. But public bathrooms were always sites of dread, and school was hard. Drucker's taste for blue hair, dog collars and makeup made her a target in Syracuse, her hometown. "She hid a lot from us," her mother, Penny Sori, told me. "It was only when I started working at the high school that I saw she took a lot of crap." When Drucker insisted on wearing a gown to the prom, her parents worried that she was putting herself at risk. But when Sori approached her, "Zackary looked at me in this funny way and said, 'I need your support on this.' So I said, 'O.K., let me find my long black gloves and at least accessorize you effectively.' "

Ernst was similarly ostracized and bullied in Chapel Hill, where his father, Carl Ernst, is an Islamic-studies professor at the University of North Carolina. As the only queer kid at his public middle school and later at the local Quaker school, he says, he was treated poorly by both students and teachers. With his parents' blessing, he dropped out in ninth grade. He studied art and music at home, set up a darkroom in his closet and took classes at local community colleges.

Art allowed them to vent their anger and defy convention. At her home, Drucker showed me a box of old photographs. Amid the pictures of her bar mitzvah ("a rare moment of gender conformity"), punk adolescence and androgynous college years was a series of snapshots from when she was 3 or 4, dressed in her mother's clothes and beaming. "Those photographs provided an opportunity for me to see myself outside of the constraints of my reality," she said. "Art-making has always provided this place to invent and reinvent myself."

Drucker went on to study photography at the School of Visual Arts in New York. Soon after arriving in the city in 2001, she met Flawless Sabrina, a revered drag performer otherwise known as Jack Doroshow, and the first of many "trans-feminine elders" Drucker collected in search of "proof that it's possible to have a sustainable life and live outside the rules." At Hampshire College, Ernst fell in love with mixed-media filmmaking, which allowed him to combine his many interests. For "The Drive North," a Super-8 short that Ernst made and starred in as a 20-year-old undergraduate, he used his own animation and original score and experimented with slide projections and energetic editing to tell a story about two teenagers driving to college. It earned him several prizes at festivals around the world. After graduation he moved to New York, where he began working as a personal assistant on film and television projects and eventually became a producer and editor on MTV.

Transitioning is a complicated and often stressful process. It took a while before it felt like a necessary step for either of them. Drucker always knew she flouted traditional gender categories, but she was able to maintain a level of androgyny until her early 20s. It was only when her body started aging in a masculine way that she realized "that wasn't the path I wanted to go down." After she moved to Los Angeles to attend the California Institute of the Arts in 2005, she began taking estrogen.

Although Ernst knew he wasn't female, transitioning made him nervous, particularly because he knew few people who had done it. "It was still this kind of distant, weird relative of 'gay and lesbian,' and people didn't understand it," he says. Without public examples of happy, successful, aging trans people, he remembered wondering: Do people grow old? Do the hormones kill you? As a feminist, he asked himself: Do I even want to be a man?

"People are afraid of saying the wrong thing, so they don't have the conversation. But I think there's no undignified questions, only undignified answers."

He was also troubled by the fact that it is impossible to transition quietly. It feels extremely public, he explains, because essentially everyone else has to transition, too. "At what point would my mom change pronouns to her hairdresser when they chat about me? It really ripples. It feels like jumping off a cliff."

Ernst began taking hormones six months before driving cross-country with a trans-male friend to study filmmaking at CalArts. They were just starting to pass as men, which meant they were "dealing with the panopticon of rest-stop men's rooms for the first time." The experience was nerve-racking, but he learned that men don't really look at one another in men's rooms. He also found that people were much kinder to him than when he was a gender-nonconforming woman. "I got the, you know, 'Sup, chief? 'Sup, champ? It was really striking."

Drucker met Ernst at a party soon after he arrived in Los Angeles. "It was such a revelation when we got together," Drucker told me. Within a year they were subletting the rundown house of Ron Athey, a performance artist and mentor (they call him "Pops"). They collaborated on several projects, including "She Gone Rogue," a dreamy experimental short featuring several "trans-feminine" legends from Drucker's "chosen family" (Flawless Sabrina, Holly Woodlawn, Vaginal Davis), which debuted at the Hammer Museum in Los Angeles in 2012. They also took thousands of pictures of themselves and each other.

The photographs that make up "Relationship" were never meant for a mass audience; Drucker and Ernst didn't even share them with friends. They feel like small, private gifts for each other. One shows them topless and tenderly touching each other in bed, their faces flushed with the thrill of discovery. Another finds them nuzzling in the dark corner of what looks like a party, their eyes closed. Often Drucker or Ernst seem to be posing for the other, preening before a mirror or gazing directly at the camera.

These photos capture them as they figure out how to present their evolving selves. Ernst is often seen gazing in the distance, steely and remote, his face sprouting new facial hair. Drucker drapes herself across the bed, feline, come-hither and increasingly curvy. Their disdain for the "prurience" of public curiosity about trans bodies mean there are no full nudes in the book. Both lament that trans people are regularly asked about their genitals. "Cis people are not asked about their genitals, so it's a bit of a double standard," Drucker says. But the photos include some comic nods. One shows Ernst with two brown eggs between his legs; another has him eating a long link of sausage impaled on a fork. Drucker is seen holding a peeled grapefruit in her lap.

As a series, these photos trace a period in Drucker's and Ernst's lives when they were both undergoing profound personal changes. Yet they found something still and stable in each other. "That body of work really speaks to how much love and support can still be at the core of something that might seem unstable or uncertain or unfamiliar," says Stuart Comer, a co-curator of the 2014 Whitney Biennial. Comer is largely responsible for making these images public. Impressed by their film "She Gone Rogue" and excited by the energy and identity politics of many trans artists, he visited Drucker and Ernst in their Los Angeles studio in 2013. Over margaritas, they shared some of their personal snapshots. Comer was so moved by them that he asked to include a selection in the Biennial.

"It was still this kind of distant, weird relative of 'gay and lesbian,' and people didn't understand it."

"The formula is so simple, but the cumulative effect of the series is extremely powerful," says Comer, who is now the chief curator of media and performance art at the Museum of Modern Art in New York. Unlike Drucker and Ernst's other collaborations, which tend to be more layered and complex, "Relationship" speaks to audiences because it is so direct. It is about love between two humans who happen to be trans.

"It's an earth-shattering book," says Kate Bornstein, a trans activist and queer theorist. "You can't read this book and not understand that trans is an identity that is desirable and filled with desire. There are going to be people writing to Zackary and Rhys saying, 'Oh, my God, thank you!' Because right now, being attracted to a trans person is seen as a perversion."

Drucker and Ernst understand why people are curious about them. "Trans people are basically asking everyone to re-evaluate their notions of gender," Drucker says. This involves more than changing a few names and pronouns. It means upending our rules about who gets to be a man or a woman, and how we expect everyone to behave. The effects can be disorienting. As someone who has occasionally chafed against the ways women are expected to perform femininity, I found myself marveling at Drucker's girlishness, including her perfectly painted fingernails (against my own hang-nailed nubs). What, I asked her, inspires these choices? Were they not burdensome? Drucker patiently explained that she does what makes her feel confident, and she likes the look of manicured nails. It was an answer that could have come from my mother.

Recognizing the difference between how gender is felt and how it is enforced can also be liberating. "Modern masculinity is so confining," Jerid Bartow, Drucker's cis-male boyfriend, told me one evening. "We're trained to swallow our emotions, to not seem like a sissy. But those expectations don't exist in our relationship, which is such a relief." Bartow recalled a night I was with him and Drucker while they were getting ready for a party, when he declared, "I'm having a clothing crisis!" next to a bed of discarded outfits. "That's something men are trained not to say."

Ernst points out that maleness does indeed come with privileges, like being able to ask for things unapologetically and say things authoritatively without being judged. But, he says, "effeminate men, gay men, smaller men, people who are perceived as younger men," don't enjoy quite the same benefits. As a 5-foot-9, sparsely bearded trans man who now identifies as gay, he says he has found it harder to secure a strong place in this "incredible pecking order." He adds that men who believe they are in male-only spaces will say "repulsive things about women." He suspects that this misogynistic posturing is largely about earning the respect of other men. "It's this male obsession with each other that results in a kind of weird, sort of insecure butt-sniffing."

Both Drucker and Ernst have made a commitment — separately and together — to live their lives as openly and proudly as possible. "As an artist, I've always believed in having a fully integrated self and not omitting parts of who you are or what your history is," Drucker says. "And being a woman named Zackary makes me very visible." Being out is not always easy. Like most trans men, Ernst passes as a cis male, so telling people he's trans means "rocking that boat every day." He recalls his discomfort during the Q.&A. sessions after screenings of his CalArts thesis short, "The Thing," at Sundance in 2012. The film is about a heterosexual couple on a fraught road trip. The man is trans. Audience members naturally asked him why he made that choice. "I realized I had to come out as trans every time on the stage," Ernst remembers. "You have to muster all this bravery and courage to transition and tell the whole world, and then you think, 'O.K., good, that's over.' But then you realize you have to continue that every day — forever."

How to Walk in High Heels

BY MALIA WOLLA | SEPT. 30, 2016

START WITH THE right shoes. Finding them should be not unlike finding a lover. "Go toward the thing that excites you the most," says Alexandra Billings, a transgender actress and theater-arts professor at California State University, Long Beach, who plays the role of mentor to Jeffrey Tambor's character on "Transparent." Billings does all her shoe shopping in brick-and-mortar stores, never online. "You've got to walk around in them, touch them, spend some time," she says. Feel even the hint of a pinched toe or wobble? Take them off. You cannot be your true self if you're in pain. Plus, Billings says, "nobody wants to see you fall."

Thicker heels are easier: You can't stand in eight-inch stilettos comfortably for as long as you can in chunky-heeled boots. Use drugstore inserts (sometimes called metatarsal pads) to further cushion the balls of your feet.

Stand up straight. Keep your chin up. Spend some time practicing. But don't obsess over mechanics. Novices worry about balance, fear missteps, fret over seeming too tall or giraffelike. But if you worry too much about tripping, you'll trip. Billings suggests that you think of high heels as existing in a sort of magnetic orbit of beauty. Step into them, and you become the gravitational center. Focus on acting the part of a graceful woman. You have to feel elegant to look it. Sometimes Billings imagines herself as the long-legged 1940s starlet Cyd Charisse.

Footwear can become important symbolically. Billings, who is 54, easily recalls the minutiae of shoes she wore at important junctures in her transition from boy to woman. The first time she wore heels, she was 7, slipping into her mother's white vinyl go-go boots while home alone playing hooky from school. "There was a great sense of power for me when I put those shoes on," Billings says. Still, don't imbue heels with too much significance. In an effort to be seen, appreciated and desired, trans females and maybe all women can overfeminize themselves, Billings says. "There was a point in my life when I realized I no longer needed heels and makeup and big hair in order to understand and represent my own feminine nature."

Hari Nef Adds Another Layer to 'Transparent'

BY KATHRYN SHATTUCK | DEC. 2, 2015

SOME WOMEN really know how to make an entrance. Consider Hari Nef, who had been in The New York Times offices for about 10 minutes before the Twitterverse issued an alert: "it's been rumored that @harinef is on the fourth floor wearing those fuzzy gucci loafers."

Ms. Nef, the first transgender model to be represented worldwide by IMG, was here to discuss her latest role: Gittel, yet another Pfefferman family secret lurking in Jill Soloway's Emmy-winning "Transparent," whose second season streams on Amazon on Dec. 11.

"I was saying it in my Instagram profile long before I was getting any work as an actress or a model," she said of her efforts to will herself into a career. "My best friend has a phrase: In New York City, if you shout something loud and long enough, it will become true."

Ms. Nef, 23, has been doing her version of shouting about transgender issues, chatting with Lena Dunham in a "Women of the Hour" podcast and visiting the White House as part of a "Champions of Change" tribute to lesbian, gay, bisexual and transgender artists.

"I used to think I was a gay man with this idea of a muse in my head, like a woman that I thought was inspirational or aspirational," Ms. Nef said, wrapping herself in a cinnamon fur-and-leather Vejas jacket. "But the woman was actually me." Here are excerpts from the conversation.

Q. *You began transitioning while a drama student at Columbia. What was that like?*

A. That was one of the most powerful experiences. Finding my new voice and my new body and a new set of roles to play, which felt so much more authentic. I always joke that I'm a better actress than I am a male actor.

Hari is a transgender model (the first to sign with IMG), actress and author who joined the cast of "Transparent" in 2015.

Q. *How did you end up on "Transparent"?*

A. Faith Soloway, Jill's sister, who writes for the show, was my camp counselor at Charles River Creative Arts Program in Dover, Mass. Jill was in New York being honored at a gala, and she emailed me out of the blue, "Do you want to be my date to this thing?" So I showed up, we hit it off, and she wrote me a part.

Q. *You play Tanta Gittel, who was mentioned in Season 1. She died in the Holocaust and left behind an heirloom ring.*

A. The family doesn't know that Gittel was born Gershon and that she lived her life as a [cross-dresser] in Berlin. Season 2 of "Transparent" sheds light on the previous generation of Pfeffermans: sibling intimacy boundary issues and gender dysphoria.

Q. *What is the show's atmosphere like?*

A. My experience with "Transparent" has completely spoiled me because it was the safest, most transpositive set ever. I didn't have to worry about all the usual things — like when people have a vision of your transness that you're not comfortable with. When they don't know the correct gender pronouns by which to refer to you. When the clothes don't fit because your body's different.

Q. *You're big on statistics. What are a few?*

A. Transpeople are unemployed at twice the national average. In 32 states, you can be denied housing and employment on the basis of being trans; 41 percent of trans teens are going to attempt suicide before the age of 18. It's so hard for many of these girls. I want to say "us." But how can I even say us when I'm so lucky and so privileged in the grand scheme of things?

Q. *In what way?*

A. I have a family that supports me, I'm financially stable, I have access to hormones.

Q. *What has been your biggest challenge?*

A. I was romantically socialized as a gay man, and now that I am, for most intents and purposes, a heterosexual woman, I have to learn how to talk to straight men, which is the scariest thing I've ever done. Being a woman means that my male privilege seeped out of my body. I'm a 2-year-old girl on a crash course.

14 TV Shows That Broke Ground With Gay and Transgender Characters

BY KATHRYN SHATTUCK | FEB. 16, 2017

LAST YEAR was a remarkable time when it came to the representation of gay, lesbian, bisexual, transgender or queer regular characters on television, according to the latest Glaad report monitoring diversity on the small screen. But that milestone, along with more accurate story lines and fewer stereotypes, has been a long time coming — a turbulent 45-year trajectory from television movies to single episodes involving secondary players to fully fleshed-out characters central to a show's story line. "All of these moments are very important in one way or another, either in progressing our lives as L.G.B.T.Q. people, or being able to help people understand who we are, especially in those times when so many people lived hidden and invisible," said Sarah Kate Ellis, the president and chief executive of Glaad (formerly known as the Gay & Lesbian Alliance Against Defamation). The following are some of the most momentous.

1972 — 'That Certain Summer' A divorced father (Hal Holbrook) hides his lover (Martin Sheen) from his teenage son in Lamont Johnson's movie for ABC, considered the first sympathetic depiction of gay people on television. (In 2015, Mr. Sheen partnered with Sam Waterston on Netflix's "Grace and Frankie.")

1977 — 'The Jeffersons' Norman Lear, who had already shaken up the staid sitcom with shows like "All in The Family" and "Maude," did so again on this CBS sitcom. In the episode "Once a Friend," George Jefferson (Sherman Hemsley) learns that his old Army buddy Eddie is now a transgender woman named Edie (Veronica Redd). (In 1975, Mr. Lear had introduced one of the first gay couples on network television in the short-lived ABC series "Hot l Baltimore.")

1977 — 'Soap' In this ABC sitcom, Billy Crystal plays Jodie Dallas — a gay man having an affair with a famous quarterback and contemplating gender-reassignment surgery — who becomes one of the first gay dads on television.

1985 — 'An Early Frost' A Chicago lawyer (Aidan Quinn) returns home to reveal to his parents that he's gay and has AIDS in this NBC movie by John Erman, setting the stage for feature films like Jonathan Demme's "Philadelphia."

1994 — 'The Real World' Pedro Zamora, the MTV reality show's first HIV-positive cast member, brings awareness to the illness and commits to his boyfriend, Sean Sasser, in the first same-sex ceremony on television.

1994 — 'My So-Called Life' In the episode "Life of Brian," this ABC drama about high school angst deals with young gay love when Rickie (Wilson Cruz) develops a crush on his new classmate, Corey (Adam Biesk).

1994 — 'Roseanne' Mariel Hemingway locks lips with Roseanne Barr in "Don't Ask, Don't Tell" — an early same-sex kiss that 30 million viewers tuned in to watch.

1996 — 'Friends' In "The One With the Lesbian Wedding," the marriage of Ross's ex-wife, Carol (Jane Sibbett), to her partner, Susan (Jessica Hecht), draws 31.6 million viewers to this NBC sitcom — even though the women don't seal their vows with a kiss.

1997 — 'Ellen' Ellen DeGeneres comes out on "The Puppy Episode" on her ABC sitcom — the first lead character to do so on television — and draws a staggering 42 million viewers. The episode also earns Ms. DeGeneres a Peabody.

1998 — 'Will & Grace' Two gay men plus two straight women equals 83 Emmy nominations and 16 wins for the show that Vice President Joseph R. Biden Jr., in 2012 on "Meet the Press," said "probably did more to educate the American public than almost anything anybody's ever done so far."

2000 — 'Queer as Folk' Showtime breaks new ground with the first hourlong drama in the United States about gay men and women, including a character who is H.I.V. positive. The cable channel does it again in 2004 with "The L Word," giving lesbians visibility they hadn't previously had.

2009 — 'Modern Family' This ABC sitcom — featuring a gay couple, Mitchell (Jesse Tyler Ferguson) and Cameron (Eric Stonestreet), and their adopted daughter, Lily (Aubrey Anderson-Emmons), as part of a larger family — "is genius in the way it integrates comedy and inclusion, and is able to educate and open people's hearts and minds," Ms. Ellis said.

2013 — 'Orange Is the New Black' This Netflix series tells the story of a women's correctional facility and its diverse cast of inmates, including the transgender Sophia (Laverne Cox) and the lesbian Poussey (Samira Wiley), who is killed off in Season 4 — the latest fatality in a 40-year string of lesbian deaths on television, beginning with Julie (Geraldine Brooks) in "Executive Suite" in 1976.

2014 — 'Transparent' This Amazon show stars Jeffrey Tambor as the patriarch of a California family who is transitioning late in life to the woman he has always identified as. Inspired by her own transgender parent, the show's creator, Jill Soloway, makes a point of putting transgender people both in front of and behind the camera.

CHAPTER 4

Pop Culture

In what might have been the most significant moment for transgender celebrities in the mainstream, in 2015, Bruce Jenner, the Olympic gold medalist and ex-partner of Kris Jenner, announced her gender transition and was introduced to the world as Caitlyn. What followed was a sea-change: the transgender movement had a significant, if complicated, protagonist. This chapter explores the coverage around Caitlyn Jenner's transition as well as the conversation surrounding transgender individuals as they have changed reality television and pop culture.

The Reluctant Transgender Role Model

BY CINTRA WILSON | MAY 6, 2011

AT THE SUNDANCE FILM FESTIVAL earlier this year, I wheedled a ticket to "Becoming Chaz," a documentary about the sex change of Chastity Bono. Having long admired the Fenton Bailey and Randy Barbato World of Wonder productions — slyly edu-taining films like "The Eyes of Tammy Faye" and oodles of just-louche-enough-for-reality-TV shows like "RuPaul's Drag Race" — I anticipated their usual mix of human interest, alternative lifestyle and salacious tabloid.

This unflinchingly personal film, which will have its premiere on Oprah Winfrey's network on Tuesday, details Chastity Bono's journey from her spangled childhood in rhinestone pantsuits on "The Sonny and Cher Comedy Hour" to a more recent two years in her televised life: Chastity, now Chaz, invited cameras to witness the searingly intimate experience of his gender transition.

Chaz, 42, and Jennifer Elia, his longtime girlfriend, must navigate his hormone injections, mood swings and personality changes, and live through a medical procedure that is part of the process of making Chaz a legal male in the State of California: he undergoes "top surgery" and has his breasts removed.

The operation is so graphic, and such a commitment — physically, emotionally and financially — that as a wincing viewer you come away with a palpable understanding of how unendurably he must be suffering in his body to want to have his own sex characteristics amputated.

Yet despite being a lifelong liberal from San Francisco and friendly with a number of transgender people, I found the film as unsettling as it was inspiring.

I came away forced to confront a whole swag-bag full of transphobias that I didn't know I'd had. So I went to Los Angeles to talk to the filmmakers, and to Chaz himself.

Just sitting on a couch with Chaz at his publicist's office is a consciousness-raising experience. He's an affable, candid, pudgy, regular guy: very sweet, very comfortable in his skin, jeans, navy blue polo shirt and simple boots. His look might seem deliberately invisible if not for his hair, which he shapes into an excellent controlled pomp that could be described as Office-Casual Elvis.

At this point in his transition, Chaz is in his "second puberty," a six- to seven-year process of hormone injections. The medical technology for genital reconstruction surgery (masculine genitoplasty, for a transgender man like Chaz) is still too new, expensive, imperfect and risky for him to opt for "bottom surgery."

"I am in a holding pattern," he said. "The payoff just isn't quite enough. I wish I had a penis, but I am O.K. for now."

At age 13, Chaz told me, he knew he was attracted to women, and assumed he was a lesbian.

"I knew my whole life something was different," he said. "As a small kid, I could be one of the boys, playing sports, fitting in. When I hit puberty, I felt like my body was literally betraying me. I got smacked everywhere with femaleness. That was really traumatic."

Realizing that he should be male took years of deduction.

"Around 2001, I started analyzing lesbians. I started to realize that even really butch-acting or -dressing women still had a strong female identity that I never had."

Though emboldened by seeing transgender people in the media, he still thought of gender-transition as the last resort of the suicidal: "I thought, transgender people are much worse off than I am. That's why they're willing to risk everything to be who they are. But the older I got, the harder it got to stay in my body."

Several scenes in the film are interviews with Cher, who I assumed would act as a guide and interpreter through this signal event in her family. Yet Cher struggles throughout the film and never quite offers a sound bite of unequivocal support for her transgender son. Seeing Cher — gay icon nonpareil — so uncharacteristically jangled raised a sticky batch of questions:

Could it be possible that the fact that Chaz is now a man is somehow Cher's fault? Did the toxic culture of celebrity damage Chastity/Chaz's gender identity? Did Cher's almost drag-queenlike hyper-female persona somehow devour Chastity's emerging femininity? Could Chaz's transition have been motivated by gender-bent Oedipal revenge? Is he reclaiming the childhood attention his superstar mother always diverted?

I had to ask: It is remotely possible that he needed to make the transition because his mom is Cher?

He gave me a warm and genuine smile.

"I don't think the way I grew up had any effect on this issue," Chaz said. "There's a gender in your brain and a gender in your body. For 99 percent of people, those things are in alignment. For transgender people, they're mismatched. That's all it is. It's not complicated, it's not a neurosis. It's a mix-up. It's a birth defect, like a cleft palate."

But being born into celebrity created a different hurdle: Chaz knew

Chaz (formerly Chastity Bono) at home in California.

he would not be able to change sexes privately. "I thought, the whole world is going to find out! How am I going to be able to live a life after that? I was scared. I believed that people were going to be actively hostile towards me."

As a "last ditch effort," he tried to live as a male but without medical intervention. It didn't work. "I feel very traditionally male," he said. "I needed a male body."

Being in-between genders, Chaz said, was far more difficult than becoming a man. He was a misfit. Now, he said, he is treated much better by people, especially men.

"I'm constantly shocked by how friendly and cool straight men are to each other. 'Hey, buddy, how's it going?' I expected to feel better and happier, but I really underestimated the impact my transition would have. I didn't realize that life could be this easy, that I could ever feel this comfortable. It was unimaginable."

In the film, Jennifer is hilariously outspoken about her ordeal, coming to terms with her lover's gender transition.

"Jenny and I had to relearn how to be together," Chaz said. "I never really understood women before, to be honest, but I had a tolerance for women that I don't have now."

I laughed. Chaz blushed.

"No, really. There is something in testosterone that makes talking and gossiping really grating. I've stopped talking as much. I've noticed that Jen can talk endlessly." He shrugged. "I just kind of zone out."

"You just don't care!"

"I just don't care!" He laughed. "I've learned that the differences between men and women are so biological. I think if people realized that, it would be easier. I would be a great relationship counselor. I know the difference that hormones really make."

Sex, for him, is completely different now. "I am completely monogamous," he said, "but I need release much more often than Jen does."

The weirdest guy thing he does now?

"I got way more gadget-oriented, I have to say. I don't know why. Definitely since transitioning I've wanted to be up on the latest, coolest toy."

In their offices on Hollywood Boulevard, Messrs. Bailey and Barbato, the directors, disabused me of the rest of my Cher-related notions.

"That's a sexy theory, but no," Mr. Barbato told me. "People don't change their sex to get back at their parents, any more than people become gay to get back at their parents."

The two men compared today's cultural blind spot regarding transgender people to attitudes about homosexuality during World War II, when homosexuals in the armed forces were considered psychiatrically abnormal and were court-martialed and dishonorably discharged. Although many in the psychiatric and transgender communities consider gender identity disorder a medical issue, it is still classified as a mental disorder by the American Psychiatric Association — a stigma that is difficult for any marginalized group to shake.

"The notion of trans is incomprehensible to most people," Mr. Bailey said. "It is so foreign."

One of the most interesting aspects of their film is the fact that although Chaz makes the physical transition, the more demanding transition, arguably, is the emotional one that everyone around him must make. There is, in essence, a death and mourning of Chastity, the woman, and an adjustment to Chaz, whom his girlfriend now compares to dating "Chastity's twin brother."

But I couldn't stop asking about Cher.

"Cher is very real in this film," Mr. Barbato said. "She's not editing herself. She's processing this majorly traumatic thing for any mother: She's struggling with the fact that her daughter has turned into a man."

Mr. Bailey brings up a fascinating moment in the film: He asks Cher a question, and she just stares, motionless and unblinking as a cobra — an excruciatingly long and pregnant pause. Then her whole posture shifts. She says, "If I woke up tomorrow in the body of a man, I couldn't get to the surgeon fast enough." Right then and there it occurs to her how to relate to it.

I bring up how uncomfortable we are as a society with people who don't fit into the usual gender roles, how they can seem unsettling on a visceral level, like a dangling participle or an unresolved chord.

"I like things that are incomplete," Mr. Bailey said. "Life is unresolvedness."

I felt slightly less lame about my own process of understanding when Rosie O'Donnell (a curator of OWN's social documentary series) told me, in a phone interview, that she, too, had to pave some inner potholes en route to accepting gender transitioning.

"As a gay woman, I found it hard to understand," she said. "I know some very masculine gay women, and I wondered if this wasn't some kind of repressed homophobia, where being straight makes it more O.K. But all of us struggle with whatever it is: special-needs kids, gay people. We all have our speed bumps."

History mostly demonstrates the violence of embracing either pole of moral certainty. The black and white of gender identification has always pushed an infinitude of differences into the margins. Who knows? To finally usher a complete color wheel of sexuality into the mainstream, perhaps it takes a child of Cher.

The Transition of Bruce Jenner: A Shock to Some, Visible to All

BY SARAH LYALL AND JACOB BERNSTEIN | FEB. 6, 2015

BRUCE JENNER has been an Olympic superstar, the hunk on the Wheaties box, a Playgirl cover boy, the author of inspirational sports books and a sometime actor and celebrity game-show contestant. In recent years, he has also been an ancillary but vivid participant in the bizarre public spectacle that is the Kardashian family.

Now Mr. Jenner, who muscled his way into American consciousness when he won the gold medal in the decathlon in the 1976 Montreal Summer Games and was anointed the World's Greatest Athlete, may be entering the newest and most surprising phase of his multi-act career. Though he has not confirmed it, he is widely reported to be in the midst of making a transition from male to female.

Other prominent people have been here before. But never has the process been played out quite like this — at the intersection where celebrity exhibitionism meets public voyeurism. Never before has it involved someone of such public ubiquity whose transition, at least so far, seems to be unfolding before our very eyes.

Dwight Stones, a former Olympic high-jump medalist who has known Mr. Jenner for years, said that his apparent transformation presented a "phenomenal opportunity."

"I think he is going to have a tremendous impact on popular culture," said Mr. Stones, who is now a broadcaster for NBC. "The parents of kids who are suppressing this, or trying to find a way to reveal themselves to the people they care about, are going to know who Bruce Jenner is. That might smooth the way or make the reality a little less difficult."

It is no secret that Mr. Jenner has been having plastic surgery procedures for many years. Kardashian followers and consumers of celebrity news have been monitoring other changes for months: his sudden hot-pink manicure, his increasingly long and bouncy hair, his new makeup regimen, his altered physique that already includes, possibly, breasts.

But for people from his early days in sports, this latest development is a shock. They remember Mr. Jenner the gifted athlete, the big personality, the charismatic wheeler-dealer who parlayed a single towering Olympic achievement into a lifetime of success and fame beyond sports.

"He was a hell of an athlete," said Keith Jackson, who covered Mr. Jenner's Olympic triumph while working as a sportscaster in 1976. "Women would stand in line just to shake his hand; young people responded to him — the Olympians at all levels, as far as I could tell. The announcer for the high jump used to give Bruce the business for being so attractive to everybody."

In recent days, Mr. Jackson said, he has talked to friends and former colleagues who competed against Mr. Jenner. "They were just like me, with their mouths open," he said.

Advocates for transgender issues declined in interviews to discuss specifics about Mr. Jenner's situation, saying that until he announces what is going on, it is wrong to make any assumptions. But at the very least, they say, his prominence has provided momentum for a continuing national discussion on the topic.

Denise A. Norris, the director of the Institute for Transgender Economic Advancement, said that the United States was going through what she called a trans-peak, with the issue often in the news.

Besides Mr. Jenner, she mentioned Laverne Cox, a transgender actress in "Orange Is the New Black," and the online show "Transparent," among other things.

"Right now we have a potential trans celebrity, and this creates a conversation," Ms. Norris said of Mr. Jenner.

There have been other prominent transgender people in recent years: Chastity (now Chaz) Bono, whose parents are Sonny and Cher; Larry (now Lana) Wachowski, a producer, director and screenwriter; and Bradley (now Chelsea) Manning, the soldier convicted of leaking classified documents in the WikiLeaks case. The most famous example in sports remains the tennis player Renee Richards, who started life as Richard Raskind, had gender reassignment surgery in 1975 and won the right to play on the women's tennis circuit.

Popular culture has indeed moved on since Ms. Richards's time.

Zackary Drucker and Rhys Ernst, two transgender artists who live together in Los Angeles, were among the most discussed participants at the 2014 Whitney Biennial. Barneys New York and the jewelry designer Alexis Bittar have both featured transgender models in recent advertising campaigns.

The memoir "Redefining Realness," by the transgender campaigner Janet Mock, became a New York Times best-seller last year. Last summer, Ms. Cox was on the cover of Time magazine, the star of an article titled "The Transgender Tipping Point."

"If we look at historic trans-peaks, we get celebrities out there — they may be great, they may be bad — but regardless of what the celebrity is doing, this creates a conversation," Ms. Norris said. "And then the activists come in and lock every bit of gain we can out of it."

Mr. Jenner's potential problems include the multitudes of people — and not just sympathetic transgender campaigners — who are trying to squeeze every bit of gain they can out of him. He has lived so long in the public eye that it will be difficult for him to harbor an expectation of secrecy now.

Not that he is seeking secrecy, at least from what is known so far. Mr. Jenner is reportedly in negotiations with Diane Sawyer over an exclusive tell-all interview. There are also talks of a reality television show about his transition.

Then there is Mr. Jenner's extended stepfamily, the Kardashians, who have their own media needs. There is the reality television show "Keeping Up With the Kardashians," which for years has followed every nuance and banality in their lives.

There are its various spinoffs, including the careers of many young women whose names start with K: Kourtney, Khloe, Kendall, Kylie and especially Kim, the ultimate Kardashian. Even though Mr. Jenner has never seemed particularly comfortable with the sturm und drang of Kardashian family life, he is implicated in it by his very presence in its midst.

Mr. Jenner and Kris, his third wife and the mother of Kim, Khloe and the rest, divorced in December. But Mr. Jenner's situation has had all sorts of familial repercussions. When he reportedly sat the family down to announce his intentions to make the gender transition, Mr. Jenner, his next reality-television project in mind, made sure that the cameras were rolling.

Marcia Ochoa, chairwoman of the feminist studies department at the University of California, Santa Cruz, said that much of the publicity swirling around Mr. Jenner, especially the obsession with his physical changes, had been ugly and prurient.

"It's such a courageous act, if she's going to be transitioning publicly and subjecting herself to that kind of ridicule," Ms. Ochoa said, using the feminine pronoun to describe Mr. Jenner. "In some ways, this is changing the whole landscape of it, because ultimately it looks inhumane, and she is a person who deserves to be happy."

RICHARD SANDOMIR CONTRIBUTED REPORTING.

Bruce Jenner Says He's Transitioning to a Woman

BY DANIEL E. SLOTNIK | APRIL 24, 2015

BRUCE JENNER, the Olympic gold medalist and member of the Kardashian family, ended months of speculation Friday night when he announced during an ABC television special that he identified as a woman and was making the transition from male to female.

"For all intents and purposes, I am a woman," he told Diane Sawyer in an interview. "People look at me differently. They see this macho male, but this female side is part of me, it's who I am. I was not genetically born that way."

The announcement made him among the highest-profile people to publicly come out as transgender. For the purpose of the interview, Mr. Jenner said he preferred the pronoun "he," and Ms. Sawyer called him Bruce. He said that he had been undergoing hormone therapy for a year and a half but had not made up his mind about reassignment surgery. He declined to provide the name he might use during or after his transition, citing privacy concerns.

Rumors about a possible transition have been trumpeted for months by tabloids and celebrity magazines.

He and his third wife, the former Kris Kardashian, who divorced in 2014, and members of the extended Kardashian family — among television's biggest reality stars — had remained coy about his plans. Kris Jenner did not comment for the special but later sent out a Twitter message supporting him. Mr. Jenner's first two wives, Chrystie Crownover and Linda Thompson, also expressed their support, as did all six of Mr. Jenner's children and his Kardashian stepchildren.

Mr. Jenner, 65, said that when he told his children, "They all cried, mainly because they don't want anybody to hurt Dad."

Mr. Jenner parlayed fame as the decathlon champion at the 1976 Summer Olympics in Montreal into a sporadic acting career that included movies like the Village People vehicle "Can't Stop the Music" in 1980. He returned to the public eye for a new generation when he became a central figure on "Keeping Up With the Kardashians," which made its debut on the E! network in 2007.

E! will also chronicle his transition in a documentary series that will begin broadcasting this summer.

With Friday night's announcement, Mr. Jenner joins transgender celebrities like the actress Laverne Cox; Lana Wachowski, who directed the "Matrix" films with her brother, Andy; and Chaz Bono, Sonny and Cher's son.

Mr. Jenner's announcement is the latest example of the growing presence of transgender people and characters on television.

There are nuanced transgender characters on scripted shows like "Orange Is the New Black" on Netflix and Amazon's Golden Globe-winning hit "Transparent," and transgender people have appeared on reality shows like "Dancing With the Stars" and "America's Next Top Model."

Several reality series, some still in the planning stages, are centered on transgender people, like TLC's "All That Jazz," about the teenage transgender activist Jazz Jennings, and VH1's "TransAmerica," about the model and activist Carmen Carrera.

Nick Adams, the director of programs for transgender media at the gay rights organization Glaad, said that any time a transgender celebrity comes forward with his or her story, "it goes a very long way toward educating people about who we are and the challenges that we face."

"Every transgender person's journey is unique, and by choosing to share this story, Bruce Jenner adds another layer to America's understanding of what it means to be transgender," Mr. Adams said in a statement on Friday night.

Mr. Adams, who is transgender, said that media portrayals of transgender people had improved since he transitioned 18 years ago. But, he said, such reports need to more fully explore what it means to be transgender.

"When the media is talking to transgender people now, they're still focused on that coming-out narrative and not very focused on giving that portrayal of transgender people as well-rounded family individuals," he said.

Mr. Jenner reflected that he had appeared in more than 400 episodes of "Keeping Up With the Kardashians" over almost eight years. He said his secret had eaten away at him all that time.

"The one real true story in the family was the one I was hiding, and nobody knew about it," he said. "The one thing that could really make a difference in people's lives was right here in my soul, and I could not tell that story."

Bruce Jenner, Embracing Transgender Identity, Says 'It's Just Who I Am'

BY ALESSANDRA STANLEY | APRIL 25, 2015

THIS WAS SHOCKING: Bruce Jenner is a Republican.

That revelation on Friday night actually was a little surprising, given that the G.O.P. is not known for embracing transgender equality. But otherwise, there wasn't much suspense to what Mr. Jenner told Diane Sawyer in his long-awaited television interview with ABC News — it has been pretty clear for some time that he identifies as a woman and has begun the transitioning process.

The doubts were not about that, but about his credibility as a champion of the transgender cause. Mr. Jenner has been such a standout in the transactional exhibitionism that is reality television that there was a risk that the coming out would seem as crass and contrived as an episode of "Keeping Up With the Kardashians."

That didn't happen. Mr. Jenner explained himself well, with passion and dignity. His emotion (he was teary at times) seemed genuine and quite touching. He told Ms. Sawyer to call him Bruce and refer to him as he, saying this was his last interview as a man. He didn't say what his name would be in future encounters, and referred to his inner self as "her."

Mr. Jenner didn't explain everything. This wasn't a confrontational interview or even a probing one: It was a careful, collaborative effort between Ms. Sawyer and her guest to turn a celebrity get into a public service announcement.

With the aid of experts and clips, ABC threaded Mr. Jenner's story with information about the transgender world, marking signs of acceptance (a Time Magazine cover and the award-winning Amazon series "Transparent") and also the vestigial stigmas that lead some people to depression, isolation and even suicide. ABC provided profiles of Christine Jorgensen and the tennis player Renee Richards.

"I'm not stuck in anybody's body, it's just who I am as a human being," Mr. Jenner said. "My brain is much more female than it is male." And while he showed Ms. Sawyer a black cocktail dress he would wear to a private dinner the two had planned, he didn't allow himself to be filmed in women's clothes — and that was the right call. Mr. Jenner explained that his femininity isn't located in his sexuality or appearance, but in his soul. There was no need to give paparazzi a tabloid shot of his new physique.

He rather sweetly said that for now, his aspirations for his new-found freedom are modest. He said he wanted to "be able to have my nail polish on long enough that it actually chips off."

This was a coming-out about gender identity and also of television genre. Mr. Jenner tried to disentangle himself from his reality show skin, shedding the slightly goofy, Father Knows Least persona he plays on E! to reveal a more forceful and assertive version of himself. He became exercised — and even sarcastic — when Ms. Sawyer told him that his Kardashian years (she only referred to the series as "that reality show") made people wonder whether this too was a publicity stunt. "Yeah, right," he drawled.

Instead, he reframed his reality show career as the price he paid to create a platform for his new calling. "Yeah, I know," he said, referring to what Ms. Sawyer described as "a shameless selling of everything." He said this was different. "But what I am doing is going to do some good and we're going to change the world. I really firmly believe that," he said shaking his finger at Ms. Sawyer. He added, "And if the whole Kardashian show and reality television gave me that foothold into that world, to be able to go out there and really do something good, I'm all for it. I got no problem with that. Understand?"

His reality show days aren't over, however. Mr. Jenner said he was doing an eight-episode documentary with E! that will air this summer but said he drew the line at giving the camera the kind of access he allowed on "Keeping Up With The Kardashians." Whatever further medical procedures he will undergo, he will do privately, without a film crew. "I'm not shooting any of this, I'm not filming anything," he said. "To me it's very degrading."

Mr. Jenner wasn't always likable in the interview, but he seemed sincere. And much of what he said about having lived a lie made sense. Mr. Jenner, who was the star of the 1976 Olympics, explained that his obsessive determination to succeed as an athlete allowed him to block out everything else. As he put it, "I didn't have to deal with me."

Mr. Jenner described himself as conservative and Ms. Sawyer seemed taken aback. When she asked him if he would ask Republican leaders to champion the transgender cause, Mr. Jenner was full of aplomb. "I would do that, yeah, in a heartbeat, why not? And I think they'd be very receptive to it."

His four children from his first two marriages participated in the interview to show their support — Brandon was especially kind, saying, "I feel like I'm getting an upgraded version of my dad."

Neither of his two daughters with Kris Kardashian nor his four famous stepchildren appeared on the show, but he said they had all come around after the initial shock, especially Kim. (It wasn't entirely a surprise to her: he said she had once caught him wearing a dress.)

He said his main concern about telling the truth was for his children, and that pain was evident. But he seemed surprisingly detached from how his ex-wives may have felt, including Ms. Kardashian. He said he had no complaints about her. Almost cavalierly, he added, "Honestly, if she would have been really good with it and understanding we'd probably still be together."

In Hollywood, the line between bravery and brazen self-promotion can blur pretty easily. Mr. Jenner took a difficult step and made the best possible case for himself while serving the cause he says he will from now on make his life's work.

"I am saying goodbye to people's perception of me and who I am," he said. "I'm not saying goodbye to me because this has always been me."

The Price of Caitlyn Jenner's Heroism

OPINION | BY RHONDA GARELICK | JUNE 3, 2015

A NEW goddess has emerged like Botticelli's Venus rising from the sea. Caitlyn Jenner gazes out from Annie Leibovitz's July Vanity Fair cover, bare save for a satin bodysuit. Her auburn curls tumble over alabaster shoulders. Can she really be the avatar of personal freedom and self-expression the media claims her to be?

Caitlyn Jenner's transition is more than a private matter. It is a commercial spectacle on an enormous scale, revealing some disturbing truths about what we value and admire in women.

Inside the magazine, Ms. Jenner poses in skintight dresses, a cinched black lace corset and two different gold evening gowns — the kind of outfits favored by her voluptuous stepdaughter, Kim Kardashian. She lounges on a sofa, peers into mirrors or reclines with her head thrown back, eyes closed. In keeping with the classic iconography of female stardom, Ms. Jenner appears languid and glamorous, her body still and on display rather than performing any activity.

Ms. Jenner is 65 years old, but Caitlyn "codes" many decades younger. Her features are tiny and doll-like, her lips plumped, her skin lineless. Even her new chosen first name feels bizarrely girlish, conjuring more a college student, or maybe a sixth Kardashian sister, than a grandmother.

We have known for months that Bruce Jenner was becoming a woman, and we rejoice if this brings her happiness. But were we prepared for this woman?

What does it mean that Ms. Jenner's newly revealed "true self" (in her own words) comes packaged like a 30-something starlet along the lines of her famous daughters and stepdaughters? She is even likened to "an elegant starlet" in the Vanity Fair profile. Like her children, Caitlyn will soon allow her life to be minutely chronicled in a reality television show, produced by the same team responsible for "Keeping Up

With the Kardashians" — that docudrama devoted to makeup, hook-ups, breakups and, of course, plastic surgery and clothes.

Long ago, Ms. Jenner was a hero, admired for dazzling athletic skills. Even on the Kardashian show, Bruce often distinguished himself as the voice of reason amid a circus of vanity and consumerism. But as Vanity Fair's Caitlyn, Ms. Jenner has morphed into a consumable commodity — a strangely static, oddly youthful and elaborately adorned body that is, rather than does. This seems less the liberation of a true self than a reminder of the straitjacket requirements of acceptable, desirable womanhood.

That Ms. Jenner makes an excellent icon of fashion is unsurprising. Not only has she long lived within the corridors of Hollywood celebrity, but her physique — still the slim-hipped, sinewy body of a male Olympic athlete — actually lends itself (with a few tweaks) more easily to the female modelesque ideal than do most genetically female bodies. And certainly, very few transwomen could achieve this aesthetic ideal either, as the actress and transgender activist Laverne Cox has pointed out in a widely read Tumblr post.

What of the millions of other 65-year-old women, whether born female or trans, who deserve attention? The millions of women who become invisible with age and could never successfully mimic a Kardashian (and would not wish to)? They remain offstage and out of mind, their own accomplishments unknown to us.

What's more, those few women of Ms. Jenner's age category who do manage to enter the public arena are routinely excoriated simply for being older — see the endless discussions on whether Hillary Clinton is "too old" to be president — or else they're shamed for trying to appear younger via cosmetic enhancement.

The French writer Simone de Beauvoir famously wrote that "one is not born a woman, one becomes one." She was referring to the innumerable embellishments, codes of behavior and self-censoring acts required by femininity, the turning of the self into a prestige commodity.

Caitlyn Jenner, center, at the Victoria's Secret Fashion Show in Manhattan in 2015.

In becoming a woman before our eyes, Caitlyn Jenner proves that little has changed since 1949, when de Beauvoir wrote those words. To be admired in the public eye, to be seen, a woman must still conform to an astonishingly long, often contradictory list of physical demands — the most important being that she not visibly age.

While the fanfare around the emergence of Caitlyn may advance our acceptance of transgender individuals, it does so, in this case, at a price: the perpetuation, even celebration, of narrow and dehumanizing strictures of womanhood sustained by the fashion and entertainment industries. True liberation of gender's vast spectrum should ask more of us than that we simply exchange one uncomfortable, oppressive identity for another.

Beyond Caitlyn Jenner Lies a Long Struggle by Transgender People

BY CLYDE HABERMAN | JUNE 14, 2015

BY NOW, most Americans are probably familiar with the rights movement known by the initials L.G.B.T., but they may have a better sense of the L.G.B. part — lesbian, gay, bisexual. The T, for transgender, has eluded many people. That, however, may be quickly changing with a string of developments in recent years, not the least being the emergence this month of Caitlyn Jenner, a transgender woman who was a public figure for four decades as Bruce Jenner, Olympic decathlon champion and reality-show personality.

"Bruce always had to tell a lie," she said in a video accompanying her appearance on the cover of Vanity Fair, but "Caitlyn doesn't have any secrets."

The Jenner story is a jumping-off point for the latest installment of Retro Report, a series of video documentaries examining major stories of the past and their enduring effects. The video, though, goes much farther back, to the 1960s and gay rights protests in San Francisco and New York. Transgender men and women, people whose sense of identity did not match the body they entered life with, played significant roles. But over the years they bore burdens unique to them, in part because they were unfamiliar to most Americans.

Though the statistics may not be fully reliable, their numbers in this country are commonly estimated at 700,000, or about three-tenths of 1 percent of the adult population. A survey of 4,509 Americans adults conducted in late 2013 by the Public Religion Research Institute found that 65 percent had close friends or relatives who were gay or lesbian. Transgender? Only 9 percent. Even so, awareness of transgender people and their issues is clearly growing, and not just because of Ms. Jenner.

Chaz Bono, the child of the entertainers Sonny and Cher; Chelsea Manning, the imprisoned leaker of Army secrets; Laverne Cox, the star of the Netflix drama "Orange Is the New Black"; writers like Jennifer Finney Boylan and Janet Mock — all are transgender men and women who are shaping the national discussion. "Transparent," an award-winning Amazon online video series, is about a family whose father is a transgender woman. Another show with a dad who is a transgender woman, "Becoming Us," began last week on the ABC Family network. On June 4, Barnard College in New York announced that it would join women's colleges like Wellesley, Mount Holyoke and Smith in enrolling transgender women.

Those sorts of developments suggest that transgender men and women have made strides toward acceptance. "We don't want anything other than our humanity," Ms. Boylan, who teaches at Barnard and is a contributing opinion writer for The New York Times, told Retro Report.

Yet hatred, discrimination and violence remain the daily lot for thousands. Seven transgender women, nearly all African-Americans, were murdered in the span of a month early this year. Suicides are common, including among teenagers, who become overwhelmed by the intolerance they face while dealing with their gender identities. In San Diego, Kyler Prescott ended his life last month at 14. In December, Leelah Alcorn, a 17-year-old in Ohio, threw herself in front of a moving tractor-trailer.

Other examples abound, and teenagers are hardly alone in struggling. A 2011 report by the National Transgender Discrimination Survey showed that an astounding 41 percent of the 6,450 people interviewed had tried to kill themselves — not just thought about it, but actually made the attempt.

The findings of the survey, titled "Injustice at Every Turn," cannot be generalized to all transgender and "gender nonconforming" people because the study was not based on a random sample. But people in the study who identified themselves as part of either of these groups said they had frequently experienced physical assaults. Transgender adults and teens who participated in the study said they were harassed in schools and on the street, sometimes by the police.

Some transgender activists feel shunted aside even by their brothers and sisters in the L.G.B.T. movement. "Trans people continue to be marginalized within the L.G.B.T. rights struggle, treated as tokens when convenient," Meredith Talusan, a transgender woman, wrote last June in The American Prospect magazine.

Life in prisons or in homeless shelters, never pleasant for anyone, can be a nightmare of rape and other abuses for transgender men and women. Lourdes Ashley Hunter, executive director of the Trans Women of Color Collective, left Detroit in 2002 to put down roots in New York. Homeless on her arrival and turned away by a women's shelter that would not accept her gender identity, she had no choice but to go to a men's shelter. There, she told Retro Report, she was raped in the shower by a man holding a razor blade.

"There was nothing that I can do," she recalled. When she reported the assault to shelter staff members, "they blamed me." And that, she said with tears welling, "is just a snapshot of what we have to go through just to live."

One goal of advocacy groups is to take control of their own narrative. "Language is power," Ms. Boylan said, echoing an understanding among political groups that a national debate on, say, a topic like the estate tax is shaped mightily by whether one calls it "a death tax" or "a Paris Hilton tax." The rights group Glaad, formed in the 1980s as the Gay and Lesbian Alliance Against Defamation, has issued a guide for news organizations filled with explanations about which words are acceptable and which are not. "Transgender," this advisory makes clear, is an umbrella term that can encompass various forms of identity. It may be applied to those who alter their bodies with hormones or through surgery and to those who make no physical changes.

As the guide also notes, the American Psychiatric Association in 2013 discarded the negative word "disorder" to describe transgender people. "Gender dysphoria" replaced a diagnosis that used to be called "gender identity disorder." The extent to which other phrases will seep into the mainstream remains to be seen. Take a word like "cisgender" — "cis" being a Latin prefix that means "on the same side as" — to describe people who are not transgender. The guide acknowledges that the term is "not commonly known outside the L.G.B.T. community."

The real point is "for people to get to know us," Nick Adams, who represents Glaad on transgender issues, told Retro Report. "And get to know that we're people just like everyone else."

Candis Cayne, From Chelsea Drag Queen to Caitlyn Jenner's Sidekick

BY JACOB BERNSTEIN | AUG. 21, 2015

LONG BEFORE Laverne Cox made the cover of Time magazine as a "transgender tipping point," and long before Caitlyn Jenner made global headlines as a former Olympian transitioning from male to female at age 65, there was Candis Cayne.

The 5-foot-10 Hawaiian beauty ruled the New York club scene for more than a decade before moving to Hollywood in 2007. There, Ms. Cayne became the first transgender actress to appear on network TV.

She was cast on ABC's "Dirty Sexy Money," opposite William Baldwin as a transgender woman having an affair with a married politician. She appeared on "Good Morning America," where Robin Roberts said she was "blazing a path" for transgender visibility.

The spotlight did not last. After "Dirty Sexy Money" was canceled, Ms. Cayne largely faded from public view. But in recent weeks she has re-emerged on a larger stage.

She appeared on the cover of Star Magazine, was interviewed by People magazine, has appeared in innumerable tabloid blog posts and was the grand marshal at the Gay Pride Parade in Montreal.

The source of this sudden attention is E!'s "I Am Cait," in which Ms. Cayne, 44, has emerged as the unlikely confidante of Ms. Jenner, accompanying her on trips to San Francisco to meet with gay and transgender activists and escorting her to the ESPY Awards in New York.

There have also been rumors of a romantic spark, though it's hard not to be skeptical that the story line was manufactured by E! producers to gin up tabloid interest. Indeed, a recent teaser posted by E! is called "Caitlyn Jenner Gets Asked Out on a Date," although the actual clip just shows Ms. Jenner going to Ms. Cayne's house for a glass of wine.

Candis Cayne ruled the New York club scene before moving to Hollywood, where she became one of the first transgender actresses to appear on network TV.

And earlier this month, Star published a photo of Ms. Cayne on its cover, with the headline: "Caitlyn Jenner: I'm in Love."

Ms. Cayne is savvy enough to know a good tabloid story, so when asked about the relationship, she simply offers, "I can say Caitlyn and I have become close, and we're great friends."

On a recent Wednesday, Ms. Cayne was running around a spacious house in the Hollywood Hills, where a photographer was taking publicity shots for her newfound fame.

There were sequins in every shade of the rainbow and dresses made out of peacock feathers. But it was her hair — long and blond and blown out to perfection, the sort beauty queens try to emulate — that completed the look.

"It's my showgirl moment," Ms. Cayne said. "This dress I'm wearing now has a kind of 'Viva Las Vegas' vibe."

Growing up in Maui in the early 1980s as Brendan McDanniel, things were a little more crunchy granola. Her parents were teachers and progressives who had few issues when, as a teenage boy, their son came out as gay. It would be several more years before Ms. Cayne came to terms with her gender identity.

Shortly after high school, Ms. Cayne moved to New York in hopes of becoming a professional dancer. She lived in a single-room occupancy hotel in the then-seedy meatpacking district; went on scholarship at Steps, a dance studio on the Upper West Side; and worked as a kitty girl at the Roxy, a former gay club in Chelsea.

"I had a tray and I would sell candy, cigarettes and lollipops," she said. "And then I realized I loved doing drag."

There, Ms. Cayne fell in with Lina Bradford, also known as the "gender illusionist" Girlina, and the two became inseparable. Ms. Cayne worked by day at the wig bar at Patricia Field's boutique in Greenwich Village, and performed by night with Ms. Bradford at Boy Bar in the East Village and the Tunnel in Chelsea.

They did triple pirouettes in four-inch pumps and knew the words to every disco song. A crowd favorite was their lip-synced rendition of "No More Tears (Enough Is Enough)," with Ms. Cayne channeling Barbra Streisand and Girlina as Donna Summer.

"They were like the Linda Evangelista and Naomi Campbell of the gay club scene," said the veteran drag performer Linda Simpson. Well, at least the scrappy downtown version of them.

Matthew Kasten, who was the promoter at Boy Bar, said, "She kept her shoes in the oven because she didn't cook."

By the time Ms. Cayne was 24, it was clear that performing in beaded gowns at night was not enough for her. "Nothing made sense," she said. "I just felt better when I was female."

But there was one thing standing in the way of a transition. "I was flat broke," Ms. Cayne said.

Through a transgender club doorwoman named Paris, Ms. Cayne began getting black-market hormones. Surgeries took place in a decrepit basement in Guadalajara, Mexico.

To help pay for her nose job, the club promoter Marc Berkley hosted a benefit at the Palladium around 1996.

"There was a dunking booth, and all the girls got in and you would pay to dunk the queens, and the money went to getting Candis a new nose," said the drag performer Sherry Vine, one of several performers who participated.

After Ms. Cayne completed her transition, she moved into the cabaret world, often performing at the Viceroy, a since-shuttered Chelsea restaurant, where her signature move was to take her show into the street, where she would continue to lip-sync and dance while climbing onto the hoods of taxicabs, as the audience watched through the plate-glass windows.

But she always wanted to act and soon began auditioning. One of her first jobs was on "CSI: NY." It was a bit part.

"I ended up getting drowned in a toilet," she said. "I was the dead person."

Then, in 2007, she received a phone call from Ms. Field, her former boss, who had since become an in-demand costume designer. Ms. Field had been hired on a noirish nighttime soap called "Dirty Sexy Money," which was casting the part of a transgender woman. Would Ms. Cayne come in and audition?

"I read for it and a week later I got a callback," Ms. Cayne said. "I had no idea it was a big deal."

But when the ratings for "Dirty Sexy Money" dropped in the second season, one of the first things that was reconsidered was her character's place in the plotline. Once again, she died an ignominious death.

"I got killed in a flashback," Ms. Cayne said. "A flashback!"

The next few years weren't easy. She got a small part on the FX show "Nip/Tuck," and appeared as a judge on "RuPaul's Drag U," an offshoot of "Drag Race."

It turns out that there weren't a lot of significant roles for transgender actresses. In recent years, she earned her living mostly by doing drag shows around the country. Meanwhile, the relationship with the man she expected to marry ended.

"I just assumed because I was a novice that I would be getting auditions and working a lot more," said Ms. Cayne, who lives in a modest home in Glendale, Calif., with her two boxers. "It was a stark reality that I faced."

Then this May, a few weeks before Ms. Jenner's Vanity Fair cover hit the newsstands, Ms. Cayne received a phone call from a producer at "I Am Cait." Except she wasn't told what the show was about.

"He said, 'I want to tell you something but I can't until you sign a confidentiality agreement,' " Ms. Cayne said. "It was like: 'Hmm. OK. I'm going to sign my life over before I know anything.' But I was also intrigued because of that."

Soon, the producer called back to say that he was working on Ms. Jenner's series for E! and that the show wanted Ms. Cayne to go to a dinner at Ms. Jenner's house.

Ms. Cayne put on a navy lace dress and drove over, and was surprised to discover not only how far along Ms. Jenner was in her transition, but that a number of other prominent trans women were there, including the artist Zackary Drucker and Jennifer Finney Boylan, a Barnard professor and frequent contributor to The New York Times.

And the cameras were rolling.

At first, Ms. Jenner was shy. "Not in the sense of being quiet," Ms. Cayne said, "but in the sense of wanting to learn. Now she's blossomed."

Likewise, a genuine friendship seems to have blossomed, on and off camera, between the two. "Very good friends" is how Ms. Cayne put it.

Perhaps eager not to alienate the producers at E! ("I don't even have a contract," she said at one point), she hedged a little when asked point blank whether she and Ms. Jenner were dating. Then she gave a wink.

"I lived in New York for 15 years," she said, alluding to the friends there who know her to be solely interested in dating straight men. "You do the math." Asked the same question on "Access Hollywood" this week, she was more direct, saying: "No. We're just really, really good friends."

If this sort of attention in the celebrity press has not bothered her, it's partly because the show has put transgender issues front and center in a way seldom seen on television.

"The reason I was like, 'Yeah, I'm going to do this' is because it's going to change the world," she said. "This is going to make a huge difference to kids who feel alone and watch this show, and see trans women who are successful, happy, amazing people."

Caitlyn Jenner's Mission

BY JENNIFER FINNEY BOYLAN | FEB. 11, 2017

DONALD TRUMP'S inauguration was devoid of stars. Elton John said no. Justin Timberlake cried the president a river. The event was barren of A-listers. Except for one.

There she was, Caitlyn Jenner, in an off-the-shoulder navy gown, cheering on the new president. "Republicans need help understanding L.G.B.T.Q. issues," she tweeted. "And I'm here to help!"

There are times when I feel like my friendship with Caitlyn is one unending Thanksgiving dinner, with me always fleeing the table in tears. But I do believe that if we're all going to survive the next four years, we have to learn not only how to talk with one another, but to listen.

Listening is no easy thing. When I spent six weeks on a bus last year with Caitlyn as part of her reality show's road trip, I asked her how she could possibly be a Republican. She replied, "Every conservative guy out there believes in everybody's rights." I shouted back, "That is a lie!" Then I hit her with a rolled-up newspaper, demonstrating exactly how bad I am at the whole listening thing.

There is, and ought to be, room for a wide range of identities within the L.G.B.T. movement. But how can queer people side with the party that has devoted much of the last quarter-century to demonizing us and opposing our rights?

As a friend once observed, queer Republicans remind him of "the pig in the chef's hat and apron holding a fork and knife on the front of a sign for a barbecue joint." Surely that pig must know that things aren't going to end well.

But Caitlyn isn't alone. According to Gallup, 21 percent of L.G.B.T. Americans are or lean Republican.

The Trump administration claims it supports gay and trans rights, as evidenced by its decision last month to preserve Barack Obama's workplace protections. "The president is proud to have been the first ever G.O.P. nominee to mention the L.G.B.T.Q. community in his nomination acceptance speech," a White House statement said.

On the other hand, this consistently inconsistent president has also said that he would "strongly consider" appointing a Supreme Court justice who would rescind the nation's marriage equality laws. And he may get his wish with Judge Neil Gorsuch. He sided with Hobby Lobby in a case that began with a fight over contraception coverage but ended at the Supreme Court with a ruling that could ultimately allow any business to discriminate against gay and trans people on the basis of religion. (A leaked draft of an executive order endorsed this same policy.) And in 2009, Judge Gorsuch rejected a transgender woman's claim that she was forced out of her job in violation of federal law.

L.G.B.T. conservatives argue that they are not "one-issue voters," that while the rights of queer Americans are important, they are not the only factor. There are a lot of issues that constitute political identity, and as it turns out, some voters feel that their own rights are not the most urgent.

I admit that I really don't get it. So in that spirit of "listening," I called Caitlyn again.

She was driving her car — "a 1960 Austin-Healey bug-eyed Sprite" — to the shop. "If we don't have a country," she told me, "we don't have L.G.B.T. issues."

I wasn't quite sure what she meant. So she went on: "It's important that we have a thriving country. I want every trans person to get a job. I want a thriving economy. I don't want massive government on top of everything we do."

Why did she go to the inauguration? "I was working," she said. "I had an objective when I went there to meet as many people and open as many doors as I possibly could, and I was able to accomplish that. Trump is really fine when it comes to these issues."

Mike Pence, she said, "is a different story." Given that he opposed the repeal of "don't ask, don't tell," and said that gay couples would cause a "societal collapse," this seemed to me like an understatement.

"Pence was happy to see me," she said. "In so many ways, we have a lot of things in common. I'm a Christian. I'm also a Republican, and I'm also trans. My faith played a very big role in what I'm doing. And I would love to explain my story to him."

As I listened, I wondered whether L.G.B.T. rights really ought not to be the most conservative of causes. Above all else we want to be left alone, without interference, to live our lives with truth and grace. What could be more conservative than that?

And yet the modern Republican Party seems to have no problem interfering with people's privacy when it comes to sexuality and gender identity. From abortion rights to opposition to marriage equality, the Republicans have advocated more government intrusion into private lives, not less.

Caitlyn is aware of this. And she warns that if there's no progress on these issues, conservatives should be prepared "for the wrath of Caitlyn Jenner coming down upon you."

Would that include voting for a Democrat?

"I could never see myself voting for a Democrat, especially right now. I think we've lost the Democratic Party. I think it has been hijacked by left-wing, radical agendas."

"Including L.G.B.T. rights?" I asked.

"Boy," said Caitlyn. "You keep going back to L.G.B.T. rights."

Yeah, I told her. I do.

I'm truly hopeful that outreach by Caitlyn — and others — will succeed, and that life will get better, for all of us.

If it doesn't? Well, you know. Enjoy the barbecue.

CHAPTER 5

Writers and Activists

For all of the inroads made by the individuals and celebrities in the previous chapters, transgender visibility has become possible because of the workings of a large and committed group of writers and activists who push the conversation and highlight the obstacles still to come. Articles in this section look at the contributions and lives of historical as well as contemporary pioneers who have devoted their lives to changing the way the world understands transgender stories.

Janet Mock Tells the Future: Trans People's Stories, and Safety on Twitter

BY ANNA NORTH | DECEMBER 18, 2014

"I BELIEVE THAT telling our stories, first to ourselves and then to one another and the world, is a revolutionary act."

So writes Janet Mock in her 2014 memoir, "Redefining Realness: My Path to Womanhood, Identity, Love & So Much More." In telling her own story of growing up as young trans woman of color, she also offers a statement of the future she would like to see. She writes of the need to "shed a light on the many barriers that face trans women, specifically those of color and those from low-income communities, who aim to reach the not so extraordinary things I have grasped: living openly and safely as my true self, holding a job, and finding love. These things should not be out of reach."

Ms. Mock's own future includes a new venture — she'll host "So Popular!," one of MSNBC's planned streaming-video shows. She talked to Op-Talk about other new developments she hopes to see in the coming years, from better protection against online harassment to a focus on trans people's lives, rather than on their transitions.

Q. *What do you hope will be different in five years' time?*

A. I think it would be a greater recognition of the lived experiences of so many of us who I think embody multiple identities. Often in feminist discourse or social justice movements, we talk about intersectionality — we all recognize it as a theory and that it represents people's lives. But I would like that to go outside of those circles. I hope in five years' time we can recognize that fact that when we say black or that when we say person of color or that when we say a trans person, we realize that these aren't just single-identity-lens people — that it's very much complicated and our discussions around the lived experiences of these people need to be just as layered.

Q. *What are you afraid will be different?*

A. My biggest fear would be health care and reproductive justice, a lot of those issues being pulled back. Particularly with women of color and with trans people, those are two vital issues. The fact that a lot of trans people and a lot of women of color don't have access to sensitive, affordable health care, and that the idea that our bodies are being policed in such a way, legislatively and also just by location and place and class and race, and all these different factors — that's what I'm very much afraid of, because if we can't determine who we are and have agency over our bodies, then I don't know how we can really take care of ourselves and exist.

Q. *What issue or event that we're talking about now will be completely forgotten in five years?*

A. Self-determination and self-definition are two things that I think we're debating heavily. Specifically in my experience as a trans woman, a lot of my conversations are around the idea of how I define my gender, how I define myself, the pronouns that I use or the name that I've chosen. I hope that we will look back on this moment and roll our eyes over a lot of the moments I've had with my interactions with people and also with media.

Q. *What kinds of interactions specifically do you hope won't be happening in the future?*

A. I hope that the conversations won't be about, "so, you were once born this way." I wish that it would be more around the idea of, "this is who you are, so let's discuss who you are and what it means to exist in your body as this person with this complicated and multilayered experience." I feel like every time we hear a trans person's story, we're often talking about where they came from, or their transition, and not so much about the idea of who they are now, and what it means to exist in that body, in that identity, now.

I think that by focusing so much on who we were born as or what people perceive us to have been assigned at birth, because we concentrate on that so much, we don't concentrate on the health care issues, the legislative issues around being able to have your gender marker change, or your name change. I hope that in five years we know who a trans person is, we know what that means, and we can talk about what it means to exist as a trans person in our culture.

Q. *What issue or event will we still remember?*

A. I feel like in the last year and a half we've had a lot of conversations specifically around trans people and culture — creating culture. I hope that in five years that's not something that's new, it'll continue to be there, tracking from Laverne Cox in "Orange Is the New Black" to "Transparent," that there will continue to be powerful stories that show the humanity of trans people, that they're part of our communities, they're part of our lives. They're not just isolated figures that we objectify in news stories, or talk about the traumas around them.

Q. *Who that you've worked with or whose work you admire will we be talking about in five years' time?*

A. I think a lot of the women that I follow on Twitter — I hope Twitter will still be here in five years, I hope it's something that's ingrained in our lives because I love it as a resource and also as a space in which I can share with people that I might not be able to see in "real life" space. I would say someone like Mia McKenzie of Black Girl Dangerous is one voice that I think is doing powerful work by creating her own publishing platform, with her book "The Summer We Got Free," or the Black Girl Dangerous anthology. I think of those works as works that I want to continue to see out there, and a lot of that came from having space on Twitter and having one's own platform and voice being heard from that particular medium.

Q. *Are there changes you hope Twitter makes in the next five years?*

A. I think that the trolling that we deal with, with little protection — I feel like we need more than the block button. There's a lot of threats that happen on a daily basis. I love the platform because it allows me to connect with people that I wouldn't otherwise see or hear from, a lot of marginalized people. And I think that the trolling that's happening there really needs to get under control, and it needs to be an even safer space for people.

Janet Mock Struggles With Being Called a 'Trans Advocate'

BY ANA MARIE COX | MAY 24, 2017

Q. *Your new book, "Surpassing Certainty," is about your 20s, and what separates it from most books about young adulthood is that you really show the messiness of becoming the person you end up being.*

A. Usually this kind of memoir comes from a grande dame — someone who's in her 60s, smoking her cigarettes and saying, "I'm going to tell the children what it was really like to fight Mr. DeMille." I'm in my mid-30s! So I am still close to the experiences, but they're far enough away for me to reflect on and to find lessons.

Q. *I think a lot of young people struggle with the process of waiting to become who they are.*

A. I get invited to a lot of college campuses, and administrators think it's going to be a lecture on "trans-ness" or whatever. But when young people get there, their questions are about just life. I was surprised by that, but then I realized that people who show up for my talks are a lot of women of color; a lot of cis-feminists; a lot of white, liberal young folk; and a lot of queer and trans people. And they're seeing, often for the first time, a reflection of the kind of life they want to live.

Q. *What do they talk to you about?*

A. None of them ask, say, how I got to where I am in my career. They're just like, "How can I show up to my internship as who I am?" I tell them how I was able to do that. I don't want them to look at me as a "fully formed person" who's being paid to talk to them, but the girl I was when I was 21 years old. I was on a pole, working. I had a sloppy boyfriend. I was borrowing my mother's car. I had all the pitfalls they had.

Q. *As a public face of the trans community, do you think that you're treated as the official representative of a marginalized group?*

A. It's one reason I'm no longer on Twitter as much as I used to be — all these things go on, and then people who are well intentioned will tweet me things asking my opinion. Like: "Can you speak out on this? Another trans woman of color has been beaten on the street." I'm not speaking about it because I'm tired of speaking about it. I'm tired of having to discuss the slices of trauma in our life that oftentimes outweigh some of the triumphs that we do accomplish. That's why I even struggle with being called a "trans advocate," because we cannot use my single experience, because all it does is flatten everyone else's experience and turns us into a monolith.

Q. *Is there a respectability politics to your role? How does it feel to be in this position?*

A. There's a burden of responsibility for me to show up correct — in my head, if I don't do it right, then I'll get shut out, and then other trans women of color will be shut out. I'm still grappling with all of that.

Q. *You engaged in sex work to earn money for your transition, which you write about frankly.*

A. The first time The New York Times wrote about me, they called me a "prostitute"! That was language I had never used in my entire life, but according to them, that is what the style guide said they needed to call me, instead of just saying "she engaged in sex work." Hopefully, in the last three years, times have changed.

Q. *After you transitioned, you worked in a strip club. In talking about this time in your life, you wrote that so much of your work involved listening and talking to customers: "crafting open roads in conversation that would stimulate him, inflate his ego and make him feel centered and listened to." Later on, you pursued a career in journalism. Do you think you learned some of those skills while employed in sex work?*

A. I never made that connection until right now. Yes, that's exactly what it is. Everyone talks about the tricks that we were doing, which was great and glamorous and looked like a Nelly video. But for clients, it was more about the quiet stuff: sitting and letting someone rub your thigh, and you nodding and listening. As a journalist, I did learn a lot there, but I also think it's just the emotional capacity to be open and vulnerable in that sense, and letting the other person lead you to a different place you didn't even know you wanted to go. You know, now I want to revise my book and make that direct connection!

Julia Serano, Transfeminist Thinker, Talks Trans-Misogyny

BY JEANNE CARSTENSEN | JUNE 22, 2017

THE BIOLOGIST, performer and author Julia Serano is a leading trans-feminist thinker and the author of "Whipping Girl," which Jill Solo-way, the creator of the Amazon series "Transparent," cites as a major influence and the first book she gives to transgender friends, like Caitlyn Jenner.

Based on Ms. Serano's experiences as a trans woman who transitioned in 2002, and deep engagement with feminist theory, her manifesto links transphobia with sexism and is a call to rethink attitudes toward femininity. She worked at the University of California, Berkeley, for 17 years doing postdoctoral research in genetics and evolutionary biology and is now a full-time writer and activist in Oakland. The following interview has been edited and condensed.

Q. One of the main ideas "Whipping Girl" became known for is "trans-misogyny." Please explain.

A. After I transitioned I experienced a combination of discrimination — for being a transgender person and also for being a woman. Trans-misogyny describes this complex interplay between transphobia and misogyny that trans women are faced with.

Q. What's an example?

A. Once in San Francisco I saw a trans woman dressed like an average feminine woman walk past a straight couple on the street. The man turned to the woman and sneered, "Did you see all that crap he's wearing?" He was referring to her dress and jewelry and makeup and all that. If a trans man had walked by, they might also have ridiculed him

Julia Serano is a writer and activist in Oakland, Calif. She transitioned in 2002 and calls herself "a femme tomboy."

for being transgender. But I doubt very much they would have made fun of his masculine clothing.

Q. *When did you become a feminist? And why?*

A. I identified as a feminist, or feminist ally, throughout my adult life. But after my transition around 2002, I began writing about my experiences with sexism as a trans woman, and that led me to become more passionate about and involved in feminism.

Q. *"Whipping Girl" is in many ways a celebration and defense of feminine gender expression. Why did you feel femininity needed a cheerleader?*

A. Some people have feminine traits or gravitate toward feminine gender expression. Historically these things have been ridiculed in comparison to masculine interests and gender expression.

If people are going to make jokes about transgender people, they usually single out trans women. The underlying theme of the joke is how ridiculous it is that someone who was a man would decide to be a woman, to be feminine. The assumption is that femaleness and femininity are inferior. That's part of the joke.

Just as feminists have long argued that women are men's equals, we should also be saying that femininity is masculinity's equal.

Q. *Most feminist and women's groups today include trans women. But there are still tensions. Recently the Nigerian novelist and feminist Chimamanda Ngozi Adichie sparked controversy with comments suggesting that trans women aren't really women.*

A. I don't think Adichie is opposed to transgender people per se. But she did go out of her way to make the case that trans women belong in a separate category.

Feminism is about putting an end to sexism, and as a feminist I personally want to see the end of sexism in all its forms: homophobia or transphobia or traditional sexism or whatever. I don't see why trans women need to be forced out into our own group separate from women in order to end sexism.

It's worth pointing out that there was a time when a lot of straight feminists similarly wanted to isolate lesbians. They accused them of being a threat to women and women's liberation. We see how wrong that was now.

Q. *Have you felt pressured to conform to certain norms of femininity?*

A. It's complicated. Just like women more generally, trans women vary a lot. Some are high femme. Some butch. I call myself a femme tomboy — I have a little of both.

But there is a sense that to be taken seriously as a trans woman, you should fit into the ideal of femininity as much as possible. Yet trans women who are very feminine are often accused of going over the top and presenting a stereotyped idea of what women should be.

A lot of my trans women friends identify as queer or lesbian so they are not canonically feminine. We are very diverse, but the trans women who get media attention tend to fit the more feminine ideal or expectations.

Q. *Do you swing optimistic or pessimistic in terms of your trans activism?*

A. In spite of the many obstacles, I tend to think we progress a little all the time. But since the election, I have been shocked at the rise of the alt-right and about how outspoken strongly sexist, racist, queer-phobic voices have become.

Q. *You began life as a male; fast-forward almost five decades and you're a trans woman feminist activist. Could you have imagined that?*

A. Not in the way you might be thinking. It's true that when I was a young boy, I couldn't have imagined I would be a trans woman. But as soon as I learned about trans people, I thought transitioning might be a possible pathway for me. But being trans has influenced me in surprising ways. Not being able to take my gender for granted from a young age forced me to become a critical thinker. And facing the obstacles of living my life as an out trans woman has made me more self-confident — not just about my trans identity, but about everything. As a young adult, I mostly saw myself as a biologist and musician, but nowadays I'm working as a writer and activist.

Q. *Do you have any sisterly advice for Chelsea Manning as she embarks on her public life as a trans woman?*

A. I don't feel comfortable addressing her or anyone specifically. But I would say to younger people in general that when it comes to trans people and transitioning, the only thing you can do is try not to let other people's expectations dictate what you do or what you become.

Leslie Feinberg, Writer and Transgender Activist, Dies at 65

BY BRUCE WEBER | NOV. 24, 2014

LESLIE FEINBERG, a writer and activist whose 1993 novel, "Stone Butch Blues," is considered a landmark in the contemporary literature of gender complexity, died on Nov. 15 at her home in Syracuse. She was 65.

Her death was confirmed by her spouse, Minnie Bruce Pratt, who said in a statement that the cause was "complications from multiple tick-borne co-infections, including Lyme disease."

Feinberg, who resisted being called Ms. or any other gender-specific honorific, wrote fiercely and furiously on behalf of those she saw as oppressed because of their sexual, ethnic, racial or other identities. A longtime member of the Workers World Party, a Marxist-Leninist group, and a prolific journalist for its newspaper, she wrote a 120-part series, from 2004 to 2008, explicating the role of socialism in the history of gender politics.

Feinberg was an advocate for minorities and for the poor, as well as for gay men and lesbians and others who identified as transgender — an umbrella term, distinct from transsexual, that describes people whose life experience straddles the line between male and female and between masculine and feminine.

She herself was biologically a woman but presented outwardly as male — and sometimes passed as a man for reasons of safety, a friend, Julie Enszer, said in an interview. Feinberg, in referring to herself, used the pronouns ze (for she) and hir (for her), though she often said pronoun usage was frequently a matter of context.

"I am female-bodied, I am a butch lesbian, a transgender lesbian — referring to me as 'she/her' is appropriate, particularly in a non-trans setting in which referring to me as 'he' would appear to resolve the social contradiction between my birth sex and gender expression and render my transgender expression invisible," she explained in a 2006 interview with Camp, a publication in Kansas City, Mo., aimed at gay, lesbian, bisexual and transgender people and their supporters.

"I like the gender neutral pronoun 'ze/hir,' " she continued, "because it makes it impossible to hold on to gender/sex/sexuality assumptions about a person you're about to meet or you've just met. And in an all trans setting, referring to me as 'he/him' honors my gender expression in the same way that referring to my sister drag queens as 'she/her' does."

Feinberg's books included two nonfiction studies of gender issues, "Transgender Warriors: Making History From Joan of Arc to Dennis Rodman" and "Trans Liberation: Beyond Pink or Blue," and a second novel, "Drag King."

But her best-known and most influential work was "Stone Butch Blues," a coming-of-age novel, drawn at least partly from her own life, about a young person, born female, who grows into adulthood at odds with her own family and comes to grips with her complicated, unconventional sexual and gender identity at a time when practicing a so-called alternative lifestyle invited stigma, open discrimination and, in many settings, menacing opprobrium.

"They cuffed my hands so tight I almost cried out," the protagonist, Jess Goldberg, writes in a letter to a former lover, describing a night the police raided a club they were in together. "Then the cop unzipped his pants real slow, with a smirk on his face, and ordered me down on my knees. First I thought to myself, I can't! Then I said out loud to myself and to you and to him, I won't! I never told you this before but something changed inside of me at that moment. I learned the difference between what I can't do and what I refuse to do."

Leslie Feinberg was born on Sept. 1, 1949, in Kansas City and grew up in Buffalo. Her family was hostile to her sexuality and gender expression, and she left home as a teenager, rejecting them as well.

According to a biographical statement supplied by her spouse, Feinberg earned a living mostly in temporary low-wage jobs, including washing dishes, working in a book bindery, cleaning out ship cargo holds and interpreting sign language.

In addition to writing, she pursued many causes as an activist. In 1974, she organized a march against racism in Boston after white supremacists had attacked blacks there. She helped rally support for AIDS patients and those at risk in the early days of the disease. A longtime advocate for women's reproductive rights, she returned to Buffalo to work for that cause in 1998, after an abortion provider, Dr. Barnett Slepian, was murdered in his home near there.

In addition to Pratt, a poet and an activist, Feinberg is survived by "an extended family of choice," according to the statement provided by her spouse. She "identified as an antiracist white, working-class, secular Jewish, transgender, lesbian, female revolutionary communist," the statement said.

In an essay after Feinberg's death, Shauna Miller, a writer and editor who contributes to The Atlantic, wrote on the magazine's website that "Stone Butch Blues" was "the heartbreaking holy grail of butch perspective," a book that was instrumental in her coming to terms with her own sexual and gender identity. The novel, which has been translated into several languages including Chinese and Slovenian, "changed queer history," she wrote.

"It changed trans history. It changed dyke history. And how it did that was by honestly telling a brutally real, beautifully vulnerable and messy personal story of a butch lesbian."

Still Here: Sylvia, Who Survived Stonewall, Time and the River

BY MICHAEL T. KAUFMAN | MAY 24, 1995

SYLVIA RIVERA, the transvestite who in 1969 battled passionately and inspirationally at the Stonewall uprising, tried to kill herself 10 days ago by walking into the Hudson River.

"I was depressed," said the 44-year-old drag queen, who had become a legendary figure of the gay political movement born on the night in 1969 when she and a few others fought back against police officers raiding the Stonewall Inn, a Greenwich Village bar. As she sat and chatted in the day room of the psychiatric wing of St. Joseph's Hospital in Yonkers, Sylvia — who always refers to herself as a woman and prefers for others to do so too — was calm.

It was Saturday and she was giving out little red doubled-over ribbons that she had made to mark the struggle against AIDS, pinning them on the other patients. She said she was sorry that she would have to miss the AIDS walk in New York City the next day. "What I've done is to get all the psychiatric patients and nurses, and we're just going to walk around this room like, you know, maybe for a half an hour."

Why did she walk into the river? She explained that she had started drinking early on that Friday. "You know, I have this problem. Well, I am an alcoholic. I drank beers and whisky right after Frank went off to work," referring to her lover of the last 15 years. "Until a week earlier we were living in a boxcar on a siding near the Yonkers train station. We were there for a couple of weeks, me, Frank and Isis, my cat.

"It was O.K., but I was feeling down about being thrown out of my apartment by people I had looked after. I had this place in Yonkers that I opened up to about 12 young queens. I was like the den mother, you know. I took them in and then they turned on me and forced me out. There's been a lot of changes for the better since I first showed up on 42nd Street when I was 11 1/2 years old, but I think these days a lot of the young people are much more cynical. People always told me I had a big heart and that I let people take advantage of it, but that's who I am."

"Well, after a few weeks the boxcar disappeared with lots of our stuff in it. Thank God I had taken Isis and boarded her with some friends. We started sleeping outside and on that Friday morning, I went down to the river to meditate. I do that usually once a day. I go down there and think about Marsha P. Johnson. Marsha was the first friend I made on 42nd street. She was 17. Marsha plugged in the light for me. Three years ago they pulled Marsha's body out of the Hudson at Christopher Street. It's still not clear whether it was suicide or if someone killed her.

"Her ashes went into the river, and I draw strength when I go down there and think about her. But that day when I was drinking I was thinking how with Marsha gone there was no one left. I thought it might be time to take a little swim. I was up to my waist when somebody saw me and the police came and brought me here.

"It's not bad here. They don't care if I do myself up, and everybody here, including the psychiatrist, calls me Sylvia. Once, years ago, I was in Bellevue, and the psychiatrist there kept telling me I was Ray. It seemed to be really important to him that I was Ray and a man," said Sylvia, who was wearing jeans. Her hair was long and mostly gray and there was only a little makeup on her face. Her handshake was strong and manly.

She has outlived the actuarial tables for her line of life, but despite the drinking, the depression and the homelessness, she was still showing plenty of attitude. Martin Duberman, the director of the Center of Gay and Lesbian Studies at CUNY Graduate Center, says she is one of the pioneers. "She has always had guts," said Mr. Duberman, the historian, who has written extensively about her. He said she deserved credit and that he would be happy to funnel help to her.

"Sylvia had a dreadful life as a child, but she overcame it and she certainly was a central figure there that night at the Stonewall. Later she was given a lot of flak from within the movement. There were gay men who were terrified of their own effeminacy, and women who were convinced that drag was mocking and stereotyping women." Banned from gay pride marches, she fought back by seizing the microphones to blister those who in search of respectability were shunning her and others like her. Outside society and outside the gay mainstream she organized a group of street transvestites who for a while lived collectively, in a rundown tenement on the Lower East Side.

But by last June, when the 25th anniversary of the Stonewall uprising was celebrated, Sylvia was restored to an honored place in the gay parades. "The movement had put me on the shelf, but they took me down and dusted me off," she recalled at the hospital. "Still, it was beautiful. I walked down 58th Street and the young ones were calling from the sidewalk, 'Sylvia, Sylvia, thank you, we know what you did.' After that I went back on the shelf. It would be wonderful if the movement took care of its own. But don't worry about Sylvia. I should be out of here in a week and I should be fine."

Marsha P. Johnson

OVERLOOKED | BY SEWELL CHAN | MARCH 8, 2018

MARSHA P. JOHNSON was an activist, a prostitute, a drag performer and, for nearly three decades, a fixture of street life in Greenwich Village. She was a central figure in a gay liberation movement energized by the 1969 police raid on the Stonewall Inn. She was a model for Andy Warhol. She battled severe mental illness. She was usually destitute and, for much of her life, effectively homeless.

When she died at 46, under murky circumstances, in summer 1992, Johnson was mourned by her many friends, but her death did not attract much notice in the mainstream press.

In the years since, however, interest in her legacy has soared. She has been praised for her insistent calls for social and economic justice; for working on behalf of homeless street youth ostracized by their families for being gay or otherwise not conforming to traditional ideas about gender; and, later, for her advocacy on behalf of AIDS patients. Some have called her a saint.

Many transgender people have also come to hail Johnson, and her longtime friend and colleague Sylvia Rivera, as pioneering heroes. (The term transgender was not in wide use in Johnson's lifetime; she usually used female pronouns for herself, but also referred to herself as gay, as a transvestite or simply as a queen.)

"Marsha P. Johnson could be perceived as the most marginalized of people — black, queer, gender-nonconforming, poor," said Susan Stryker, an associate professor of gender and women's studies at the University of Arizona. "You might expect a person in such a position to be fragile, brutalized, beaten down. Instead, Marsha had this joie de vivre, a capacity to find joy in a world of suffering. She channeled it into political action, and did it with a kind of fierceness, grace and whimsy, with a loopy, absurdist reaction to it all."

Johnson was born Malcolm Michaels Jr. on Aug. 24, 1945, in Elizabeth, N.J., the fifth of seven children in a working-class family. Her father, Malcolm Michaels Sr., worked on the assembly line at a General Motors factory in Linden. Her mother, the former Alberta Claiborne, was a housekeeper.

Johnson was around 5 when she began to wear dresses, but felt pressure to stop because of other children's aggression. Later, Johnson said in an interview toward the end of her life, she was sexually assaulted by another boy, who was around 13.

She began attending the Mount Teman African Methodist Episcopal Church as a child and practiced her Christian faith throughout her life; later, she was drawn to Catholicism and visited houses of worship of other faiths frequently. She graduated from Thomas A. Edison High School in Elizabeth in 1963, and promptly moved to New York City, she later recalled, with $15 and a bag of clothes.

It was not an easy time to live outside the sexual mainstream. Although New York State downgraded sodomy from a felony to a misdemeanor in 1950, persecution of gay people and criminalization of their activities were still common. Same-sex dancing in public was prohibited. The State Liquor Authority banned bars from serving gay people alcoholic beverages. People could be charged with sexual deviancy for cross-dressing. Police enforcement was often arbitrary.

After arriving in New York, Johnson alternated between going by her given name, Malcolm, and a persona she had created, Black Marsha. She engaged in prostitution and was often arrested — she stopped counting after the 100th time, she later said — and was once, in the late 1970s, even shot. She could often be found in seedy hotels near Times Square, including the Dixie Hotel (now the Hotel Carter) on West 43rd Street.

"The ones that used to make the most money was the boys that could wear their own hair, with just a little bit of makeup," she later recalled.

Johnson was a key figure in the disturbances that followed a police raid at the Stonewall Inn, a gay bar on Christopher Street, early in the morning of June 28, 1969. Many legends have grown around the event — often characterized as a riot, but more recently described as a rebellion or uprising — but the evidence suggests that Johnson was among the "vanguard" of those who resisted the police, according to David Carter, the author of "Stonewall: The Riots That Sparked the Gay Revolution." She was 23 at the time.

Stonewall helped to galvanize a more assertive, even militant, gay-rights movement. It prompted the first gay pride parades, in 1970. The same year, Johnson joined Rivera in founding Street Transvestite Action Revolutionaries, or STAR, to advocate for young transgender people — and, for a time, house, clothe and feed them, from a tenement at 213 East Second Street. STAR grew out of the Gay Liberation Front, which advocated for sexual liberation and pushed to align gay rights with other social movements.

Her goal, she declared in an interview for a 1972 book, was "to see gay people liberated and free and to have equal rights that other people have in America," with her "gay brothers and sisters out of jail and on the streets again." She added, in a reference to the radical politics of the time, "We believe in picking up the gun, starting a revolution if necessary."

The 1970s were a time of greater visibility for Johnson. Tall and slender, she had a knack for commanding attention. Her outfits — red plastic high heels; slippers and stockings; shimmering robes and dresses; costume jewelry; bright wigs; plastic flowers and even artificial fruit in her hair — were often assembled from scavenged or discarded materials.

"I was no one, nobody, from Nowheresville, until I became a drag queen," she said in a 1992 interview.

Among those who noticed was Warhol. He took Polaroids of Johnson and included her in "Ladies and Gentlemen," a 1975 portfolio of screenprints depicting drag queens and transgender revelers at The Gilded Grape, a nightclub. Johnson was also part of a drag performance group, Hot Peaches, that began performing in 1972. She told anyone who asked — including, once, a judge — that her middle initial stood for "pay it no mind." The surname came from a Howard Johnson's restaurant where she liked to hang out.

Yet life was never easy for Johnson. She had the first in what she said was a series of breakdowns in 1970, and was in and out of psychiatric institutions after that. ("I may be crazy, but that don't make me wrong," she often said.) She was generally known for her warmth and charisma, but she also could get into physical scraps and be frightening to others.

"She would wander, start off talking about one thing and end up miles away; people would say that drugs had ruined her mind, that she was a permanent space cadet," the historian and author Martin Duberman wrote in "Stonewall," adding that Johnson's mind had "concentrated wonderfully" when she was organizing STAR.

In 1980, a pivotal year for Johnson, she was invited to ride in the lead car of New York's annual Gay Pride Parade, and began living at the home of a close friend, the gay activist Randy Wicker, in Hoboken, N.J. She cared for Wicker's lover, David Combs, before he died of AIDS, in 1990. Grieving for friends, she could sometimes be found prostrate before a statue of the Virgin Mary at the Catholic Community of Saints Peter and Paul in Hoboken. She was also an AIDS activist, attending protests by and meetings of ACT UP, the AIDS advocacy organization.

In a June 26, 1992, interview, Johnson said she had been H.I.V.-positive for two years. "They call me a legend in my own time, because there were so many queens gone that I'm one of the few queens left from the '70s and the '80s," she said.

Several days later, she was seen for the last time. On July 6, 1992, her body was pulled from the Hudson River, near the Christopher Street piers. Her death was quickly ruled a suicide, a determination that many of her friends and acquaintances questioned.

Later in 1992, the authorities reclassified the cause, to drowning from undetermined causes, and in 2012, they agreed to take a fresh look at the case, which officially remains open.

Johnson has been the subject of several film projects, including work by Reina Gossett and Sasha Wortzel and documentaries in 2012 by Michael Kasino and in 2017 by David France. France's film, "The Death and Life of Marsha P. Johnson," focused in part on the efforts of Victoria Cruz, a transgender activist and a volunteer with the New York City Anti-Violence Project, to investigate the case.

Johnson's ability to mix flamboyant joy with determined activism is a central part of her legacy.

"As long as gay people don't have their rights all across America," she once said, "there's no reason for celebration."

SEWELL CHAN IS AN INTERNATIONAL NEWS EDITOR AT THE TIMES.

Bathroom Case Puts Transgender Student on National Stage

BY SHERYL GAY STOLBERG | FEB. 23, 2017

WASHINGTON — The bespectacled teenager in the gray A.C.L.U. hoodie and cargo pants stood, back pressed against a chain-link fence on Pennsylvania Avenue, under a sign saying "No Trespassing, Authorized Personnel Only." The White House, illuminated at night, cast a glow over well-wishers who, having just wrapped up a protest against President Trump, waited in line to pay homage to 17-year-old Gavin Grimm.

Mr. Grimm looked a little flustered. "Absolutely humbled," he pronounced himself, as his admirers thanked him for being brave.

With Mr. Trump's decision this week to rescind protections for transgender students that allowed them to use bathrooms corresponding with their gender identity, the next stop is the Supreme Court, where Mr. Grimm — an engaging yet slightly awkward young man — is the lead plaintiff in a case that could settle the contentious "bathroom debate."

Amid a thicket of conflicting state laws and local school policies on bathroom use, the suit, which pits Mr. Grimm against his school board in Gloucester County, Va., could greatly expand transgender rights — or roll them back.

Mr. Trump has portrayed the issue as one of states' rights, and already the country's transgender students face differing realities depending on their school. Some are restricted to the bathroom of the gender on their birth certificate. Others are not. Then there are the students like Mr. Grimm, who have had separate facilities set aside for them.

At issue in Mr. Grimm's case is whether Title IX, a provision in a 1972 law that bans discrimination "on the basis of sex" in schools that receive federal money, also bans discrimination based on gender

AL DRAGO/THE NEW YORK TIMES

Gavin Grimm, 17, a transgender student with a lawsuit before the Supreme Court next month, was embraced by Vanessa Ford, whose daughter is transgender, at a rally outside the White House on Wednesday.

identity. President Barack Obama concluded that it did. Despite Mr. Trump's action, lawyers for both Mr. Grimm and the school board said Thursday that they expected the case to go forward, with oral arguments set for March 28 and school officials across the country awaiting the result.

"No one was in a rush to bring this case to the Supreme Court," said Joshua Block, a lawyer with the American Civil Liberties Union, which represents Mr. Grimm. "Gavin didn't choose this fight; this fight happened to Gavin. But now that we are here, lives are at stake, and they are at stake in a way that is even more acute because you don't have a federal government anymore to protect us."

For Mr. Grimm, who said he knew he was a boy "as soon as I was aware of the difference between boys and girls," the case amounts to a crash course in government and media relations. It bears his initials, G.G., because he is a minor, and the name of his mother, Deirdre.

WRITERS AND ACTIVISTS **177**

At home in rural Gloucester, he is a kid with a pet pig named Esmeralda, a geek's love of Pokémon cards and 600-plus Facebook friends. He wears $12 sneakers from Walmart and likes eating at Fuddruckers because the name sounds funny. He is applying for college, but doesn't want to talk about it.

But here in the nation's capital and in big cities around the country, Mr. Grimm is now a hot property, the new face of the transgender rights movement. Laverne Cox, the actress and activist, gave him a public shout-out at the Grammys. ("Everyone, please Google 'Gavin Grimm,' " she said.) After his appearance here Wednesday night, he dashed off to New York to appear Thursday morning on ABC's "The View."

At the protest here Wednesday night, he was the star speaker, besieged with teary hugs and cellphone selfies. The mother of a transgender child burst into tears when she saw him. A government lawyer shook his hand. Activists posed for pictures.

Suddenly, he is hearing his name mentioned in the same breath as Norma McCorvey, the eponymous plaintiff in Roe v. Wade, the Supreme Court case that established a national right to abortion (and who died last week), and Jim Obergefell, whose case led to the legalization of same-sex marriage.

Mr. Grimm looked awe-struck at the thought. "I just hope I do it justice," he said quietly.

When Mr. Grimm was about 12 or 13, he said, he was able to put a name to what he was feeling and recognized himself as transgender. He came out first to his friends, which was easier than telling his parents.

For the family, it was a jolt, his mother said. It made her question preachers — she eventually left her church — but strengthened her faith.

"God gave me this child to open my heart and my mind," Mrs. Grimm, a nurse, said.

In 2014, when Mr. Grimm was 15 and starting his sophomore year, the family told his school he was transgender. Administrators were supportive at first and allowed him to use the boys' bathroom.

But amid an uproar from some parents and students, and after two tense school board meetings, the board barred Mr. Grimm from using the boys' bathrooms and instead adopted a policy requiring transgender youth to use separate "single user" restrooms. The school now has three such restrooms, but two are in refurbished utility closets, said Mr. Block, the A.C.L.U. lawyer.

Kyle Duncan, a lawyer for the school board, said the board "agonized" as it sought a thoughtful way to accommodate Mr. Grimm while protecting students who felt uncomfortable. "This is a sensitive and difficult issue in which everyone's privacy rights need to be respected," he said.

But Mr. Block said that Mr. Grimm had been singled out for "classic sex discrimination."

Mrs. Grimm was more pointed: "This school board has targeted my child."

Her son did not always have such aplomb. Before he began "living authentically," his mother said, he was introverted, often retreating to his room. She winces at the times she tried to curl his hair and make him wear dresses.

Mr. Grimm is, by all accounts, the perfect plaintiff, poised beyond his years. He knows how to deflect unwanted lines of questioning (he will not talk about his twin brother, friends or teachers) and is unfailingly polite in replying to intimate queries about his bathroom habits ("If I have to go, I go to the nurse's restroom," he told a local television reporter on Wednesday night) and his emotions ("It's incredibly frustrating, it's embarrassing, it's very uncomfortable. I have this neon sign above my head that says I'm different from my peers").

But at heart, he is still a kid. Once, while touring the National Archives here, Mr. Grimm excitedly played Pokémon Go in front of the Declaration of Independence, as Bill Farrar, a spokesman for the A.C.L.U.'s Virginia affiliate, patiently tried to remind him that he was probably "the only person here who has a legal proceeding before the Supreme Court."

The two have bonded over hours of travel, including a dash from Gloucester to Washington on Wednesday. Mr. Grimm stuffed his belongings in a white trash bag, sticking in a dress shirt at the last minute, which proved handy for "The View."

Because Mr. Grimm is to graduate this year, it is unlikely that he will benefit if the court finds in his favor. And legal experts say that is a big if. The Supreme Court could rule narrowly, send the case back to the appeals court for further review, or decide to wait until similar suits percolate through the federal court system.

And with just eight justices on the court — confirmation hearings for Judge Neil M. Gorsuch, Mr. Trump's nominee for the ninth seat, are scheduled to begin March 20 — the justices might be inclined to wait.

"There are many reasons not to resolve this issue now," said Carl Tobias, a professor at the University of Richmond School of Law, who has followed the case.

But Vanita Gupta, who ran the Civil Rights Division in Mr. Obama's Justice Department and helped write the directive that Mr. Trump rescinded, said the Grimm case had already advanced the cause of transgender rights, just by raising awareness.

"There has been such social and cultural change in the hearts and minds of people in this country," she said, "and I think that's only going to grow, even if there is a legal setback."

Whatever happens, Mr. Grimm appears destined for a life of advocacy. He says he feels a heavy burden standing up for other transgender people, knowing that everyone is different. He worries that other young people will not have the support that he has had.

While he is not much on school (he is taking only the two courses he needs to graduate), he would like to be a geneticist. He wants to know how the brain works.

But asking him about his career plans brings a Gavin-like answer — wry and pointed.

"I want to be," he said, "someone who doesn't have to talk about where he is going to use the bathroom."

Gavin Grimm: The Fight for Transgender Rights Is Bigger Than Me

OPINION | BY GAVIN GRIMM | MARCH 7, 2017

JUST OVER TWO YEARS AGO, I started my sophomore year of high school. The summer before, I had come out to my family and friends as a transgender boy. I also came out to the school administration, telling them who I was and asking them to respect my gender identity. They assured me that teachers and administrators would call me Gavin, and use male pronouns when referring to me, and if anyone gave me any kind of trouble, it would be resolved right away. By the time I started school, I had legally changed my name and I was poised to start testosterone.

However, I was still anxious. I come from a fairly conservative community, and I wasn't sure that I'd be accepted for who I am. Because of this anxiety, I did not ask permission to use the boys' restroom. I was not yet accustomed to advocating for myself, and I worried that I would be asking for too much, too soon. Instead, I used the restroom in the nurse's office.

The office was far away from my classrooms that year. It took far too much time out of my day to use the restroom, especially when, in any class, I was just down the hall from a perfectly good boys' room. So I approached the administration again. This time, I asked to use the bathrooms that correspond to my gender identity. My principal told me the following day that I was free to use the boys' restrooms, and I did. For a period of roughly seven weeks, I went in and went out with no altercations of any kind. No physical or verbal confrontation. No restroom misconduct by or against me. This seven-week period showed me what it was like to be embraced by your school, and it gave me confidence that I would be able to live out a normal school year, unencumbered by restroom politics.

Gavin Grimm, center, at a rally outside the White House in February.

This was, unfortunately, a false sense of security. After that seven-week period, the school board held a meeting — a public conversation about my genitals and restroom usage — without notifying me first. My mother and I found out by chance less than 24 hours before the meeting was to happen. An old friend of my mother's had noticed a post going around Facebook, a rallying cry by adults in my community urging people to show up to the meeting in order to "keep that girl out of the boy's room."

I went to the meeting, in November 2014, and spoke at it. Family and a few friends stood by me, but nothing could have prepared that insecure 15 year old for what was to come. People speaking out against me made a point of referring to me with female honorifics and pronouns. They warned me that I was going to be raped or otherwise abused. They suggested that boys would sneak into the girls' room and harm their children. At a second meeting, a month later, the rhetoric was even more inflammatory. Word had spread throughout the community and people turned up in droves. After each frenzied remark, clapping and hollering reverberated throughout the room. I sat while people called me a freak. I sat while my community got together to banish a child from public life for the crime of harming no one. I sat while my school board voted to banish me to retrofitted broom closets or the nurse's restroom.

And then it was over. At least it felt like it, back then. I was back to being exiled. I heard sneers and whispers about me in the hallways. My school board had invalidated me in perhaps the most humiliating way possible.

But two years later — two crazy, stressful, busy, breathtaking, rewarding, beautiful, fantastic years later — I stand stronger and prouder than ever. I stand not only with my family and friends, but with millions of supporters who stand with me. I stand with so many wonderful people at the A.C.L.U. that I proudly call my family. I know now what I did not know then; I will be fine. Regardless of what obstacles come before me, regardless of what hatred or ignorance or discrimination I face, I will be fine, because I have love on my side.

This case will not be resolved until after I graduate. But this fight is bigger than me. I came to realize that very early on, and it is truer now than it ever has been. This fight is for other trans youth in my high school. It is for other trans youth in Virginia. It is for all trans youth who are in school or one day will be. It is for the friends and loved ones of these youth, who want these children to be happy and healthy, rather than at risk and in danger as so many trans people are.

I am often asked if I regret my actions, or if I would do anything differently if I had the chance. When people ask that, I immediately think about the hundreds of parents who have reached out to thank me on behalf of their children. I think of the hundreds of young people who have thanked me themselves. I think of the countless #StandWith-Gavin messages on social media, and the countless hugs and handshakes at school and on the sidewalks of my town. I think of people I've gotten to meet and grown to love. I think of how honored I am to carry the voice, in some way, of a community so rich and so colorful and so important. I think of how I've grown from that 15-year-old child, sitting in fear as he waits to hear what his future will be, into the young man who stands hand in hand with a huge community as we all prepare to take the next step in this fight. I think of my parents, unwavering and strong as pillars in my success and growth. And I say, "Absolutely not."

GAVIN GRIMM IS A SENIOR AT GLOUCESTER HIGH SCHOOL IN VIRGINIA.

'I Am a Female,' Manning Announces, Asking Army for Hormone Therapy

BY EMMARIE HUETTEMAN | AUG. 22, 2013

WASHINGTON — One day after being sentenced to 35 years in prison for leaking vast archives of secret government files to WikiLeaks, Pfc. Bradley Manning said Thursday that he was female and that he would seek hormone therapy, setting up a potential conflict over a treatment the Army said it does not provide its inmates.

In a statement read on the "Today" show during an appearance by his lawyer, David E. Coombs, Private Manning said he had always felt he was female, something that was discussed during his court-martial.

"As I transition into this next phase of my life, I want everyone to know the real me," the statement said. "I am Chelsea Manning. I am a female. Given the way that I feel, and have felt since childhood, I want to begin hormone therapy as soon as possible. I hope that you will support me in this transition."

Mr. Coombs said Private Manning had decided to wait to speak publicly about his gender identity until after the sentencing.

Lt. Col. Stephen Platt, an Army spokesman, said the Army did not provide hormone therapy or gender-reassignment surgery. As is the case for all soldiers, transgender inmates are eligible for psychiatric care, he said.

Mr. Coombs acknowledged as much on "Today." He said that his client had not signaled an interest in gender-reassignment surgery, but that he was hopeful that the prison at Fort Leavenworth, Kan., where Private Manning will be held, would "do the right thing" and provide hormone therapy. Such regimens can help people with male physical features become more feminine.

Mr. Coombs said that if military officials did not provide hormone therapy willingly, "then I'm going to do everything in my power to make sure they are forced to do so."

A spokesman at Fort Leavenworth said he was not sure an inmate would be allowed to undergo hormone therapy, even if he could cover the cost on his own.

Neal Minahan, a Boston lawyer who has represented gay, lesbian and transgender prisoners, said they had a right to medical care — including hormone therapy used in gender reassignment — that has been consistently upheld by the courts.

Prisons generally offer three arguments against providing hormone therapy, Mr. Minahan said. They say psychotherapy and antidepressants are sufficient medical care; they question the underlying diagnosis; or, most commonly, they contend that hormone therapy could threaten the safety of transgender inmates, putting them at a higher risk of assault.

Mr. Minahan said he knew of several inmates undergoing hormone therapy, some of them for more than a decade, who have not encountered problems in the general prison population. Hormone therapy would not compromise Private Manning's safety because he has gone public about his gender identity, he said.

"It's already out there," Mr. Minahan said. "The stigma attached to it and the risk of assault within the prison population is already there, and hormones don't add to that."

The Fort Leavenworth spokesman said inmates there were still soldiers and, as such, wore uniforms and were expected to maintain a professional military appearance, which includes refraining from growing out their hair.

The 450 or so prisoners, all of whom are men, do not share cells, the spokesman said.

When asked on "Today" whether Private Manning's ultimate goal was to be housed in prison with women, Mr. Coombs said, "No, I think the ultimate goal is to be comfortable in her skin and to be the person that she's never had an opportunity to be."

Defense lawyers raised the fact that Private Manning is transgender during the sentencing phase of his courtmartial describing the emotional stress he endured while deployed in Iraq.

Two psychiatrists testified about treating Private Manning for gender identity disorder, a diagnosis for psychological discomfort with one's sex that the American Psychiatric Association renamed gender dysphoria last year. The psychiatrists said handling such a diagnosis in a combat zone, and at a time when it was still against military rules to be openly gay, would have put Private Manning under immense pressure.

"You put him in this environment, this kind of hypermasculine environment, if you will, and with no supports and few coping skills, the pressure would have been difficult to say the least," Capt. Michael Worsley, a clinical psychologist who treated Private Manning, said in court last week. "It would have been incredible."

According to testimony, Private Manning e-mailed a photograph of himself dressed in a blond wig and makeup to a supervisor at one point during his deployment. In the e-mail, which he titled "My Problem," he described a struggle with something that "makes my entire life feel like a bad dream that won't end."

The Bradley Manning Support Network, a grass-roots activist group that has raised money for Private Manning's defense, asked supporters last year to refer to him using the masculine pronoun until he expressed a preference. "Everything we know from Bradley Manning's friends, family, and legal defense team, is that he wishes to be referred to as Brad or Bradley until he's able to get to the next stage of his life," the statement said.

In an online conversation published by Wired magazine's Web site in 2010, Private Manning told the man who eventually turned him in to the authorities, Adrian Lamo, that "I wouldn't mind going to prison for the rest of my life, or being executed so much, if it wasn't for the possibility of having pictures of me plastered all over the world press as a boy."

Why I'm Ambivalent About Chelsea Manning

OPINION | BY JENNIFER FINNEY BOYLAN | JAN. 18, 2018

"WE LIVE IN TRYING TIMES," Chelsea Manning says in a video released over the weekend announcing her candidacy for the Senate, taking on Benjamin Cardin of Maryland in the Democratic primary. "Times of fear. Times of suppression."

Her unsettling spot is replete with footage of white supremacists executing Nazi salutes, police in riot gear carrying off protesters — all the atrocities of the Trump era in which we are now mired. These alternate with shots of a leather-clad Ms. Manning walking determinedly in the nation's capital, a red rose in her hand. She is poised, but she is angry and ready for a fight (starting with the Democratic Party, of which Senator Cardin is one of its most powerful figures).

It's impossible to look at that video without thinking of the civil rights and antiwar movements 50 years ago. So many of its images remind me of ones I've seen before — police attacking black people with fire hoses, marches on Washington, a young person gently putting a flower in the muzzle of a soldier's gun.

Then, as now, it was unclear whether the best way to confront our enemies was to fight them or forgive them. Then, as now, it was unclear whether the best way to bring about social change was through violence or love. For me, Ms. Manning's candidacy — in fact, her whole career in the public eye — brings that confusion to a sharp point.

When I came out as transgender in 2001, advocates in the generation before mine frequently told me: "The only way to survive your life as a public advocate is to never let people see your rage or your tears. You have to be above reproach. You have to be Jackie Robinson."

I tried, in my own meager way, to follow the example of Brooklyn's 42. As I embarked on my own career as a public person, I too tried to be above reproach, smiling forgivingly as a student at a university in

Ohio attempted to compliment me by saying, "You know, Professor, before I heard your lecture, I used to think people like you should be, you know, exterminated."

I laughed along with a studio audience when Oprah Winfrey sang to me, "Yes, she has a vagina, she has a vagina today!"

Later, off camera, I'd curl up into a ball and weep, thinking of the words of Clarence the Angel: "There must be an easier way of winning my wings." What I did not do was fight back.

Ms. Manning is an angrier public figure than I am, but she has good reason to be angry. For violating the Espionage Act, she served seven grisly years in prison, much of it at Fort Leavenworth — a military facility for male offenders, in spite of having publicly declared her female identity on the day after her conviction. During her incarceration, which ended after President Barack Obama commuted most of her sentence in January 2017, she endured a hunger strike and a suicide attempt. I can't imagine the horrors she has experienced, and my heart truly goes out to her. If I'd been through all that, I'd be angry too.

At the same time, I'm not sure she's the senator Maryland needs right now. And it's not just me — some of the people most ambivalent about Chelsea Manning are other transgender people, and our veterans not least. Kristin Beck, a former Navy SEAL who took an unsuccessful run for Congress herself two years ago, said in 2013 that Ms. Manning was a traitor: "What you wear, what color you are, your religion, race, ethnicity, sexual orientation, gender identity has no basis on whether you are a criminal or not."

It is possible to have opposed George W. Bush's war in Iraq and to nonetheless condemn Ms. Manning for leaking classified documents in the effort to end that war. It is possible to enthusiastically advocate equality and justice for L.G.B.T. Americans and to nonetheless wonder whether Ms. Manning is the best messenger for that fight.

In spite of my suspicion that Ms. Manning is not the ideal candidate, I nonetheless admire her willingness to put herself out there in the rough world of national politics. And I also worry for her, in the same way I worry for anyone who places their transness at the center of a public identity. Since coming out as transgender, I have often wondered whether being trans was the thing that hindered my career as a writer, or the thing that made it possible.

In part, I wish for Chelsea Manning the thing I sometimes wish I had chosen for myself — a life of privacy and quiet instead of a life in which you have to sit there smiling on television while a celebrity sings a song about your vagina. But maybe Ms. Manning will also find what I've found — that progress is its own reward, and that the loss of a private life is a small price to pay in exchange for justice.

I'm not sure she has my vote. But whether she wins her wings, or not, she has my respect.

JENNIFER FINNEY BOYLAN (@JENNYBOYLAN), A CONTRIBUTING OPINION WRITER, IS A PROFESSOR OF ENGLISH AT BARNARD COLLEGE AND THE AUTHOR OF THE NOVEL "LONG BLACK VEIL."

Ben Barres, Neuroscientist and Equal-Opportunity Advocate, Dies at 63

BY NEIL GENZLINGER | DEC. 29, 2017

BEN BARRES, a neuroscientist who did groundbreaking work on brain cells known as glia and their possible relation to diseases like Parkinson's, and who was an outspoken advocate of equal opportunity for women in the sciences, died on Wednesday at his home in Palo Alto, Calif. He was 63.

In announcing the death, Stanford University, where Dr. Barres was a professor, said he had had pancreatic cancer.

Dr. Barres was transgender, having transitioned from female to male in 1997, when he was in his 40s and well into his career. That gave him a distinctive outlook on the difficulties that women and members of minorities face in academia, and especially in the sciences. An article he wrote for the journal Nature in 2006 titled "Does Gender Matter?" took on some prominent scholars who had argued that women were not advancing in the sciences because of innate differences in their aptitude.

"I am suspicious when those who are at an advantage proclaim that a disadvantaged group of people is innately less able," he wrote. "Historically, claims that disadvantaged groups are innately inferior have been based on junk science and intolerance."

The article cited studies documenting obstacles facing women, but it also drew on Dr. Barres's personal experiences. He recounted dismissive treatment he had received when he was a woman and how that had changed when he became a man.

"By far," he wrote, "the main difference that I have noticed is that people who don't know I am transgendered treat me with much more respect: I can even complete a whole sentence without being interrupted by a man."

Dr. Barres (pronounced BARE-ess) was born on Sept. 13, 1954, in West Orange, N.J., with the given name Barbara.

"I knew from a very young age — 5 or 6 — that I wanted to be a scientist, that there was something fun about it and I would enjoy doing it," he told The New York Times in 2006. "I decided I would go to M.I.T. when I was 12 or 13."

Barbara did indeed go to the Massachusetts Institute of Technology on a scholarship, graduating in 1976 with a degree in life science, then moving on to Dartmouth Medical School and receiving an M.D. there in 1979.

Dr. Barres became interested in the degeneration of brain function during an internship and residency at Weill Cornell Medical College and returned to school to study it, this time at Harvard Medical School, receiving a Ph.D. in neurobiology there in 1990.

A postdoctoral fellowship took Dr. Barres to University College London and the lab of Dr. Martin Raff, who was studying glia, the cells in the human brain that are not nerve cells. Dr. Barres went to Stanford in 1993, taking his interest in glia with him. In 2008 he became chairman of the neurobiology department.

"Ben pioneered the idea that glia play a central role in sculpting the wiring diagram of our brain and are integral for maintaining circuit function throughout our lives," said Thomas Clandinin, a professor of neurobiology at Stanford who assumed the chairmanship in April 2016 when Dr. Barres's cancer was diagnosed. "People had thought glia were mere passive participants in maintaining neural function. Ben's own work and that of his trainees transformed this view entirely."

Dr. Barres and researchers working with him studied the three types of glial cells and their role in proper neonatal brain development, as well as the possibility that inflamed glia are a cause of neurodegenerative disorders. Stanford said Dr. Barres published 167 peer-reviewed papers in his career.

To many, though, just as important as his research was his willingness to speak out on sexism and related issues. He called for more day-care support for women in the sciences who also wanted families. He criticized tenure systems that seemed weighted against women. He was furious at male colleagues who bragged about having sex with their female students.

But he also faulted women for being part of some of these problems — particularly women who succeeded despite the obstacles and then acted to protect their hard-won turf.

"Accomplished women who manage to make it to the top may 'pull up the ladder behind them,' " he wrote in the Nature article, "perversely believing that if other women are less successful, then one's own success seems even greater."

His objections to the innate-differences arguments brought him criticism, with some arguing that he was trying to stifle unfashionable ideas in a way contrary to the academic tradition of open discussion. He disagreed sharply.

"When faculty tell their students that they are innately inferior based on race, religion, gender or sexual orientation," he wrote, "they are crossing a line that should not be crossed — the line that divides free speech from verbal violence."

He did not disagree that there are differences between male and female brains, but did object to the interpretation.

"People are still arguing over whether there are cognitive differences between men and women," he told The Times. "If they exist, it's not clear they are innate, and if they are innate, it's not clear they are relevant."

Or, as he put it in a 2015 letter to The Times prompted by an article about Caitlyn Jenner, "The question is not whether male or female brains are different, but why society insists on labeling male brains as better."

He is survived by a brother, Donald, and two sisters, Jeanne and Peggy.

To convey that the playing field is often not level for women pursuing careers in math and science, Dr. Barres would sometimes recount an incident from his college days, when he was still Barbara.

"An M.I.T. professor accused me of cheating on this test," he told The Times. "I was the only one in the class who solved a particular problem, and he said my boyfriend must have solved it for me. One, I did not have a boyfriend. And two, I solved it myself, goddamn it!"

Japanese Transgender Politician Is Showing 'I Exist Here'

BY MOTOKO RICH | MAY 19, 2017

IRUMA, JAPAN — In addition to his name and title, the business card of Tomoya Hosoda, a city councilman in a suburb of Tokyo, bears a unique description.

"Born a woman," it reads.

Mr. Hosoda, 25, won his seat on the City Council in conservative-leaning Iruma in March, becoming the first openly transgender man elected to public office in Japan and one of only a handful around the world.

Japan has not experienced the kind of transgender moment that has swept the United States, where the politics of sexual identity have convulsed schools, popular culture and big-time sports in recent years.

The appearance of transgender Japanese television stars may convey the illusion of a culture at ease with gender fluidity. But this is a country where transgender people must be labeled as having a mental disorder in order to legally transition from one sex to the other, and where transgender people can struggle to rent apartments, obtain medical care or hold jobs.

Mr. Hosoda thinks that in his small way, he can make an important contribution simply by being public and confident about his identity, particularly for young people who may be confused about their own.

"I wanted to show children in elementary or junior high school that I exist here," he said in an interview in the Iruma office of the Democratic Party, which Mr. Hosoda represents on the Council. "I strongly felt that way, and that's why I entered politics."

Mr. Hosoda himself benefited from the activism of Japan's only other transgender politician, Aya Kamikawa, who has sat on the council in Setagaya, a ward of Tokyo, for 14 years.

Ms. Kamikawa, a transgender woman, lobbied for a change in Japan's law to allow transgender people to officially change their gender on the all-important family registry certificate that every Japanese citizen must hold, and that is often needed to rent an apartment or receive medical care or other services.

Under that law, only people who have received a diagnosis of "gender identity disorder" and have undergone sexual reassignment surgery may legally change their gender. Activists say the law makes it difficult for those who are transitioning or do not want surgery to live or work as the gender with which they identify and often leads to discrimination by those who recognize only biological gender.

In Mr. Hosoda's case, growing up as a girl named Mika in Iruma she never met anyone who was transgender and did not even know it was possible to transition from female to male.

All she knew was that she did not feel like a girl. She hated being forced to wear a skirt as part of her uniform in high school. When it came time for her coming-of-age ceremony at age 20, she balked at having to wear a feminine kimono.

Through an internet connection, she met a man who had transitioned from a woman, opening her eyes to the possibility of another life path. This mentor encouraged her to come out to her parents.

Anxious about how they would respond, she wrote a letter and handed it to her mother in the parking lot of a supermarket. She feared that if she handed over the letter at home, she would just run to her room rather than face her mother's reaction.

Mr. Hosoda, who was then studying to be a medical technician, recalled that after his mother read the letter, the first words out of her mouth were "I'm so sorry." She was devastated to learn that her daughter had been suffering in silence for so long, and wanted to offer her child her full support as daughter transitioned to son.

In 2014, Mr. Hosoda underwent sexual reassignment surgery, which allowed him to convert his gender on his official family register.

By the time he decided to run for office, he felt comfortable going public with his identity, although his appearance could have allowed him to disguise his past. With his carefully moussed, close-cropped hairstyle, black-and-silver wire glasses and hints of a beard, he resembles many other men in their 20s in Tokyo.

His campaign brochures noted prominently that he is a transgender man, and he advocated a platform of embracing diversity, not just for sexual minorities but also for the elderly, children and people with disabilities.

Mr. Hosoda did not experience any discrimination during the campaign, he said. He squeaked onto the Council, receiving the second-fewest votes among the 22 members elected.

In Iruma, Shinji Sugimura, director of the local chapter of the Democratic Party, said Mr. Hosoda had succeeded because "he didn't push his thoughts to others but tried to be understood first."

"He's good as a politician rather than an activist," Mr. Sugimura added.

Ms. Kamikawa, who recalls being harassed during her first run for office 14 years ago, said she was heartened that Mr. Hosoda had not faced the kind of attacks she had. Some people hurled epithets, she said, and others asked, "What kind of parents raised someone like you?"

Some transgender activists say that even as Japanese society has grown more superficially accepting of transgender people, many hurdles remain.

People who prefer not to risk surgery for health reasons or who are still in the process of changing their biological sex live in a limbo where they are not allowed to live as they choose.

"When someone points out that their appearance doesn't match their official family register, they need to explain themselves each time," said Yuka Tateishi, a lawyer who is representing a transgender woman fighting for the right to use the bathrooms that correspond to her gender identity at work.

Takamasa Nakayama, founder of a transgender support organization in Japan, said some people had been fired after coming out.

"Sometimes they are discriminated against because their appearance is changing," Mr. Nakayama said. "If you are not strong enough, it's hard to keep a full-time job and survive the bullying."

Japanese national health insurance does not cover gender reassignment surgery or hormone therapy, and there are few doctors in Japan with such expertise. And the Education Ministry recently declined to add content about transgender issues to its curriculum for kindergarten and elementary and junior high schools, arguing that such discussions would be "difficult " because of challenges in "achieving the understanding of parents and the public."

In Iruma, Mr. Hosoda said he hoped to establish a counseling service at City Hall where teenagers grappling with their gender identity could seek guidance. He noted that the suicide rate among such teenagers was three to four times as high as it was for those who were not questioning their gender identity.

Even if Mr. Hosoda mainly focuses on the bread and butter of public life, like making sure the streetlights work, experts on gender issues in Japan say he could be a potent symbol.

"If the only openly transgender people on television are entertainers, the public is being presented with a very skewed version of reality which may not contribute to broader acceptance," said Gill Steel, associate professor at Doshisha University. "Hopefully, politicians who are transgender and are simply doing a good job in the public eye will increase mainstream tolerance."

Above all, said Mr. Hosoda, in a society that values conformity, "I want to give a message that you are O.K. the way you are."

He added, "You don't have to make yourself or put yourself into a certain mold."

MAKIKO INOUE CONTRIBUTED REPORTING.

Danica Roem Wins Virginia Race, Breaking a Barrier for Transgender People

BY MAGGIE ASTOR | NOV. 7, 2017

SHE CAMPAIGNED ON everyday issues, like reducing traffic on a congested state highway. But her victory on Tuesday was a social breakthrough that brought seasoned advocates to tears.

In a local election in Northern Virginia, Danica Roem, 33, defeated a Republican who had served in the state's House of Delegates for a quarter of a century — and, in doing so, Ms. Roem became the first transgender person to be elected to the Virginia legislature.

Only one other openly transgender person has been elected to a state legislature anywhere in the United States: Stacie Laughton, a Democrat who won a seat in the New Hampshire House in 2012 but never took office because of an outcry over her failure to disclose a felony conviction. Another, Althea Garrison, elected to the Massachusetts House in 1992, came out as transgender during her term in office but lost every campaign she ran after coming out.

Ms. Roem and her campaign manager, Ethan Damon, did not respond to an email requesting comment Tuesday evening. But in a recent interview with Mother Jones, Ms. Roem emphasized that her campaign was about policy, not just her identity.

"Transgender people have really good public policy ideas that span the gamut of transportation policy to health care policy to education policy, and yes, to civil rights as well," she said. "We shouldn't just be pigeonholed into the idea that we're just going to be fighting about bathrooms."

Ms. Roem will be just one state lawmaker out of more than 7,000 nationwide, but her victory resonated far beyond her legislative influence.

Danica Roem campaigning in Manassas, Va., last month.

Gay and lesbian Americans have made major strides in terms of both social acceptance and political representation, but transgender Americans are still struggling for both. There are seven openly gay members of Congress — six in the House and one in the Senate — but no openly transgender members. Many antidiscrimination laws protect people on the basis of sexual orientation but not gender identity, and killings of transgender people are on the rise.

But in January, Sarah McBride, a spokeswoman for the Human Rights Campaign, tweeted, "a trans woman will walk into the capitol built by Jefferson to take her seat in the Virginia legislature."

In an email on Tuesday night, Ms. McBride, herself a transgender woman, wrote: "It's difficult to encapsulate just how powerful it is to see this particular glass ceiling shattered. Reading the history books growing up, it became clear to me that no one like me made it very far — at least no one who was out."

"For trans youth across the country, Danica Roem's election isn't just a headline or even history," she added. "It's hope. Hope for a better tomorrow."

Charles Clymer, a writer who identifies as genderqueer, tweeted that Ms. Roem had "inspired a generation of trans kids to believe."

The symbolism of Ms. Roem's victory was amplified by the fact that the man she defeated — Bob Marshall, a Republican running for his 14th term — is an outspoken opponent of transgender rights. He introduced a bill this year that would have barred transgender students from using the bathrooms of their choice and required school officials to inform the parents of any student who asked "to be recognized or treated as the opposite sex." And during the campaign, he repeatedly used male pronouns to refer to Ms. Roem.

In a Facebook post after the race was called, Mr. Marshall thanked his supporters and wrote, "Though we all wish tonight would have turned out differently, I am deeply grateful for your support and effort over the years." He did not mention Ms. Roem.

Ms. McBride predicted that more openly transgender candidates would run for office now that Ms. Roem has paved the way.

"And if they're greeted by skeptical party leaders or operatives," she said, "they can point to Roem's victory as proof that trans candidates can win, that their candidacies can generate excitement, and that voters will judge trans candidates on their merits, not their identities."

The Modern Trans Memoir Comes of Age

BY JENNIFER FINNEY BOYLAN | JUNE 13, 2017

IF ALL LIFE is revision, then what do the memoirs of transgender people tell us about the process of creating the best draft of the self? Two new books — Caitlyn Jenner's "The Secrets of My Life" (written with Buzz Bissinger) and Janet Mock's "Surpassing Certainty" — provide some answers.

Trans people have always been part of humanity, but it's only in the last century that we've begun to tell our own stories. In this country, you can find a record of our existence as far back as the portrait of Viscount Cornbury, a colonial governor of New York and New Jersey. A painting hanging in the New-York Historical Society shows the governor in a lovely formal gown and tiara, holding an ornamental fan. He said he represented Queen Anne in America and that "in all respects I ought to represent her as faithfully as I can."

The modern trans memoir came into being with Christine Jorgensen's "A Personal Autobiography," published in 1967. Jorgensen's transition was covered with all the subtlety of a Martian invasion; "Ex-G.I. Becomes Blonde Bombshell" ran a typical tabloid headline. To read the book now is to see how dearly Jorgensen wished to be understood, even as she seemed aware of how resistant some of her readers might be.

It's a common theme in trans memoirs, the hope of being known. It runs through other early canonical works, such as "Conundrum" (1974), by the legendary travel writer Jan Morris, and "Second Serve" (1983), by the tennis great Renée Richards. The authors seem to be on the defense at times and write as if the question of their humanity were part of an argument they might win or lose. They're not much concerned with gender theory; Morris once said, "When I hear the word 'gender,' I reach for my pistol." Instead, they dwell on transition and its many permutations: medical, social and hormonal.

It was Kate Bornstein's "Gender Outlaw," originally published in 1994 and revised last year, that radically reconfigured the genre. Bornstein — actor, provocateur, gleeful troublemaker — playfully mixed memoir and gender theory, and popularized the idea that gender isn't a binary. Many people find their best, true selves somewhere between the extremes of male and female, she wrote (the subtitle to her book is "On Men, Women, and the Rest of Us"). In her revision, Bornstein wished to correct her thesis that we must do away with gender entirely. "If I used to say binary = bad, and nonbinary = good, I've since come to believe that in fact, both binary and nonbinary, as ways of being, are good," she told me. "Whatever people need to do to find their happiness, as long as they're not mean, is fine with me."

Bornstein paved the way for books like Jamison Green's "Becoming a Visible Man" (2004), the first great memoir by a trans man. Green takes an explicitly intersectional angle and echoes some of the gender theory that made "Gender Outlaw" so unnerving — and so entertaining.

Where do the books by Mock and Jenner (both of whom I know) fall in this tradition? "Surpassing Certainty" is partly in the mode of "Gender Outlaw," and positions its story within a larger history of a struggle for human rights. But Mock's book is also a work of the heart, much of it focusing on the dissolution of her first marriage, and her journey from a Honolulu strip club to an editor at People magazine.

Jenner, who didn't come out until after she was eligible for Social Security, has a very different story to tell. Much of her book is about the millstone of celebrity; it's more Chaz Bono ("Transition," 2011) than Kate Bornstein. In my own memoir, "She's Not There," I wrote that the biggest change in life was not going from male to female but going from a person with secrets to a person without them, and Jenner shares this plaint. But she's found peace at last: "The more we celebrate our difference, the more we will be celebrated," she writes. "There are too many of us out there anyway just waiting to bloom."

I like to tell people, "If you've met one trans person, you've met … one trans person"; the diversity of experience within our community is what I find most important. Unlike the writers who've come before, Mock and Jenner are freed from the burden of pioneering the genre. And it isn't their trans identities that make their stories worth reading. It's their courage and grace — qualities that are, of course, neither male nor female, but human.

Maybe the memoirs in this blossoming genre teach us that trans experience is a more vivid version of something universal. After all, is there anyone who hasn't carried something secret in her heart and wondered if she could summon the courage to bring it into the light? Or wondered if she could draft a better, truer version of herself? Could there ever be anything more human than the desire to be known?

Stories of transgender people, as harrowing as they can be, remind us that with cunning, imagination and luck, we are sometimes able, against all odds, to create — and revise — our own souls. I wonder what Lord Cornbury would think now about the territory he once called home.

Glossary

androgynous Having the characteristics of both male and female.

assigned male/female at birth Because gender is a wholly internal sense of one's identity and completely unrelated to an individual's anatomical features, gender is considered "assigned" or "designated" at birth.

bigotry Intolerance toward those who hold different opinions from oneself.

cisgender A person whose gender matches the sex they were assigned at birth.

gay Men expressing a sexual or romantic preference for other men, or more generally attraction to people of the same sex or gender.

gender dysphoria A medical term to describe the distress or depression produced by a gap between one's gender identity and their assigned birth gender.

gender identity A person's perception of one's own gender. It may or may not correlate with the assigned sex at birth.

gender-queer Relating to a person who does not identify with conventional gender distinctions.

intersectionality The interconnected nature of categorizations such as race, class, and gender as they relate to overlapping systems of discrimination.

lesbian A woman who expresses a sexual or romantic preference, but only for other women.

marginalization The treatment of a person or group as insignificant or unimportant.

misgender To refer to someone using a pronoun that does not correspond to the gender they identify as.

transgender man A person who identifies as a man but was assigned female at birth.

transgender woman A person who identifies as a woman but was assigned male at birth.

transition To adopt permanently the outward or physical characteristics of the gender with which one identifies, as opposed to those associated with one's birth sex.

transphobia Fear, aversion to, or discrimination against transgender people.

visibility The state of being seen; the level to which something has attained prominence or attention.

Media Literacy Terms

"Media literacy" refers to the ability to access, understand, critically assess, and create media. The following terms are important components of media literacy, and they will help you critically engage with the articles in this title.

angle The aspect of a news story that a journalist focuses on and develops.

attribution The method by which a source is identified or by which facts and information are assigned to the person who provided them.

balance Principle of journalism that both perspectives of an argument should be presented in a fair way.

bias A disposition of prejudice in favor of a certain idea, person, or perspective.

byline Name of the writer, usually placed between the headline and the story.

caption Identifying copy for a picture; also called a legend or cutline.

chronological order Method of writing a story presenting the details of the story in the order in which they occurred.

column Type of story that is a regular feature, often on a recurring topic, written by the same journalist, generally known as a columnist.

commentary Type of story that is an expression of opinion on recent events by a journalist generally known as a commentator.

credibility The quality of being trustworthy and believable, said of a journalistic source.

critical review Type of story that describes an event or work of art, such as a theater performance, film, concert, book, restaurant, radio or television program, exhibition, or musical piece, and offers critical assessment of its quality and reception.

editorial Article of opinion or interpretation.

fake news A fictional or made-up story presented in the style of a legitimate news story, intended to deceive readers; also commonly used as an insult to criticize legitimate news that one dislikes because of its perspective or unfavorable coverage of a subject.

feature story Article designed to entertain as well as to inform.

headline Type, usually 18 point or larger, used to introduce a story.

human interest story Type of story that focuses on individuals and how events or issues affect their lives, generally offering a sense of relatability to the reader.

impartiality Principle of journalism that a story should not reflect a journalist's bias and should contain balance.

intention The motive or reason behind something, such as the publication of a news story.

interview story Type of story in which the facts are gathered primarily by interviewing another person or persons.

inverted pyramid Method of writing a story using facts in order of importance, beginning with a lead and then gradually adding paragraphs in order of relevance from most interesting to least interesting.

motive The reason behind something, such as the publication of a news story or a source's perspective on an issue.

news story An article or style of expository writing that reports news, generally in a straightforward fashion and without editorial comment.

op-ed An opinion piece that reflects a prominent journalist's opinion on a topic of interest.

paraphrase The summary of an individual's words, with attribution, rather than a direct quotation of their exact words.

plagiarism An attempt to pass another person's work as one's own without attribution.

quotation The use of an individual's exact words indicated by the use of quotation marks and proper attribution.

reliability The quality of being dependable and accurate, said of a journalistic source.

rhetorical device Technique in writing intending to persuade the reader or communicate a message from a certain perspective.

source The origin of the information reported in journalism.

sports reporting Type of story that reports on sporting events or topics related to sports.

style A distinctive use of language in writing or speech; also a news or publishing organization's rules for consistent use of language with regard to spelling, punctuation, typography, and capitalization, usually regimented by a house style guide.

tone A manner of expression in writing or speech.

Media Literacy
Questions

1. Identify the various sources cited in the article "Transgender Models Find a Home" (on page 27). How does the journalist attribute information to each of these sources in their article? How effective are their attributions in helping the reader identify their sources?

2. In "Jackie Shane, a Transgender Soul Pioneer, Re-emerges After Four Decades" (on page 76), Reggie Ugwu paraphrases information from and directly quotes Doug McGowan. What are the strengths of the use of a direct quote as opposed to a paraphrase? What are its weaknesses?

3. Compare the headlines of "Just Being Himself, in a Professional Women's Hockey League" (on page 16) and "Transgender Man Is on Women's Team" (on page 10). Which is a more compelling headline, and why? How could the less compelling headline be changed to draw better the reader's interest?

4. What type of story is "The Price of Caitlyn Jenner's Heroism" (on page 137)? Can you identify another article in this collection that is the same type of story?

5. Does Cintra Wilson demonstrate the journalistic principle of impartiality in their article "The Reluctant Transgender Role Model" (on page 120)? If so, how did they do so? If not, what could they have included to make their article more impartial?

6. The article "Why I'm Ambivalent About Chelsea Manning" (on page 189) is an example of an op-ed. Identify how Jennifer Finney Boylan's attitude, tone, and bias help convey their opinion on the topic.

7. Does "Who Gets to Play the Transgender Part?" (on page 37) use multiple sources? What are the strengths of using multiple sources in a journalistic piece? What are the weaknesses of relying heavily on one source/few sources?

8. What type of story is "Transgender Models Find a Home" (on page 27)? Can you identify another article in this collection that is the same type of story?

9. "Janet Mock Tells the Future: Trans People's Stories, and Safety on Twitter" (on page 153) is an example of an interview. What are the benefits of providing readers with direct quotes of an interviewed subject's speech? Is the subject of an interview always a reliable source?

10. What is the intention of the article "Beyond Caitlyn Jenner Lies a Long Struggle by Transgender People" (on page 140)? How effectively does it achieve its intended purpose?

11. Analyze the authors' bias in "The Price of Caitlyn Jenner's Heroism" (on page 137) and "Caitlyn Jenner's Mission" (on page 150). Do you think one journalist is more biased in their reporting than the other? If so, why do you think so?

12. "Laverne Cox: 'Blending In Was Never an Option' " (on page 93) is an example of an interview. Can you identify skills or techniques used by Erik Spitznagel to gather information from Laverne Cox?

13. Identify each of the sources in "Japanese Transgender Politician Is Showing 'I Exist Here' " (on page 196) as a primary source or a secondary source. Evaluate the reliability and credibility of each source. How does your evaluation of each source change your perspective on this article?

14. What type of story is "Ben Barres, Neuroscientist and Equal-Opportunity Advocate, Dies at 63" (on page 192)? Can you identify another article in this collection that is the same type of story?

Citations

All citations in this list are formatted according to the Modern Language Association's (MLA) style guide.

BOOK CITATION

NEW YORK TIMES EDITORIAL STAFF, THE. *Transgender Activists and Celebrities.* New York: New York Times Educational Publishing, 2019.

ARTICLE CITATIONS

ASTOR, MAGGIE. "Danica Roem Wins Virginia Race, Breaking a Barrier for Transgender People." *The New York Times*, 7 Nov. 2017, www.nytimes.com/2017/11/07/us/danica-roem-virginia-transgender.html.

BARNES, BROOKS. "Who Gets to Play the Transgender Part?" *The New York Times,* 3 Sept. 2015, www.nytimes.com/2015/09/04/movies/who-gets-to-play-the-transgender-part-in-hollywood.html.

BERNSTEIN, JACOB. "Candis Cayne, From Chelsea Drag Queen to Caitlyn Jenner's Sidekick." *The New York Times*, 21 Aug. 2015, www.nytimes.com/2015/08/23/fashion/caitlyn-jenner-candis-cayne-i-am-cait.html.

BERNSTEIN, JACOB. "In Their Own Terms: The Growing Transgender Presence in Pop Culture." *The New York Times*, 12 Mar. 2014, www.nytimes.com/2014/03/13/fashion/the-growing-transgender-presence-in-pop-culture.html.

BERNSTEIN, JACOB. "Last Night, Calvin Klein — This Morning, Algebra." *The New York Times*, 8 Sept. 2017, www.nytimes.com/2017/09/08/fashion/calvin-klein-ariel-nicholson-murtagh-new-york-fashion-week.html.

BOBROW, EMILY. "How Two Producers of 'Transparent' Made Their Own Trans Lives More Visible." *The New York Times*, 13 Sept. 2016, www.nytimes.com/2016/09/18/magazine/how-two-producers-of-transparent-are-making-trans-lives-more-visible-starting-with-their-own.html.

BUCKLEY, CARA. "An Oscar-Nominated Transgender Director on His 'Authentic Self.' " *The New York Times*, 20 Feb. 2018, www.nytimes.com/2018/02/20/movies/transgender-director-oscar-strong-island-documentary.html.

BUCKLEY, CARA. "Transgender, and Embraced, on the Red Carpet." *The New York Times*, 9 Dec. 2015, www.nytimes.com/2015/12/10/movies/transgender-and-embraced-on-the-red-carpet.html.

CARSTENSEN, JEANNE. "Julia Serano, Transfeminist Thinker, Talks Trans-Misogyny." *The New York Times*, 22 June 2017, www.nytimes.com/2017/06/22/us/lgbt-julia-serano-transfeminist-trans-misogyny.html.

CHAN, SEWELL. "Marsha P. Johnson." *The New York Times*, 2018, www.nytimes.com/interactive/2018/obituaries/overlooked-marsha-p-johnson.html.

COX, ANA MARIE. "Janet Mock Struggles With Being Called a 'Trans Advocate'." *The New York Times*, 24 May 2017, www.nytimes.com/2017/05/24/magazine/janet-mock-struggles-with-being-called-a-trans-advocate.html.

DREIER, FREDERICK. "For Transgender Triathlete, a Top Finish in New York Is Secondary." *The New York Times*, 5 Aug. 2011, www.nytimes.com/2011/08/06/sports/for-transgender-triathlete-a-top-finish-is-secondary.html.

FINNEY BOYLAN, JENNIFER. "Caitlyn Jenner's Mission." *The New York Times*, 11 Feb. 2017, www.nytimes.com/2017/02/11/opinion/sunday/caitlyn-jenners-mission.html.

FINNEY BOYLAN, JENNIFER. "The Modern Trans Memoir Comes of Age." *The New York Times*, 13 June 2017, www.nytimes.com/2017/06/13/books/review/critics-take-queer-writing.html.

FINNEY BOYLAN, JENNIFER. "Why I'm Ambivalent About Chelsea Manning." *The New York Times*, 18 Jan. 2018, www.nytimes.com/2018/01/18/opinion/chelsea-manning-senate.html.

GARELICK, RHONDA. "The Price of Caitlyn Jenner's Heroism." *The New York Times*, 3 June 2015, www.nytimes.com/2015/06/03/opinion/the-price-of-jenners-heroism.html.

GAY STOLBERG, SHERYL. "Bathroom Case Puts Transgender Student on National Stage." *The New York Times*, 23 Feb. 2017, www.nytimes.com/2017/02/23/us/gavin-grimm-transgender-rights-bathroom.html.

GENZLINGER, NEIL. "Ben Barres, Neuroscientist and Equal-Opportunity Advocate, Dies at 63." *The New York Times*, 29 Dec. 2017, www.nytimes.com/2017/12/29/obituaries/ben-barres-dead-neuroscientist-and-equal-opportunity-advocate.html.

GRIMM, GAVIN. "Gavin Grimm: The Fight for Transgender Rights Is Bigger Than Me." *The New York Times*, 7 Mar. 2017, www.nytimes.com/2017/03/07/opinion/gavin-grimm-the-fight-for-transgender-rights-is-bigger-than-me.html.

HABERMAN, CLYDE. "Beyond Caitlyn Jenner Lies a Long Struggle by Transgender People." *The New York Times*, 14 June 2015, www.nytimes.com/2015/06/15/us/beyond-caitlyn-jenner-lies-a-long-struggle-by-transgender-people.html.

HAIGNEY, SOPHIE. "To Play Transgender, Sandra Caldwell Had to Open Up About Who She Is." *The New York Times*, 28 Aug. 2017, www.nytimes.com/2017/08/28/theater/to-play-transgender-sandra-caldwell-had-to-open-up-about-who-she-is.html.

HAWGOOD, ALEX. "Meet Jaimie Wilson, a Transgender Activist With Guitar in Hand." *The New York Times*, 26 Jan. 2018, www.nytimes.com/2018/01/26/style/jaimie-wilson-transgender-activist-musician.html.

HIGGINS, MATT. "Just Being Himself, in a Professional Women's Hockey League." *The New York Times*, 19 Oct. 2016, www.nytimes.com/2016/10/20/sports/hockey/harrison-browne-transgender-hockey-player.html.

HUETTEMAN, EMMARIE. " 'I Am a Female,' Manning Announces, Asking Army for Hormone Therapy." *The New York Times*, 22 Aug. 2013, www.nytimes.com/2013/08/23/us/bradley-manning-says-he-is-female.html.

KAUFMAN, MICHAEL T. "Still Here: Sylvia, Who Survived Stonewall, Time and the River." *The New York Times*, 24 May 1995, www.nytimes.com/1995/05/24/nyregion/about-new-york-still-here-sylvia-who-survived-stonewall-time-and-the-river.html.

KRUEGER, ALYSON. "Transgender Models Find a Home." *The New York Times*, 3 Mar. 2017, www.nytimes.com/2017/03/03/fashion/transgender-models-casting-agencies-fashion-week.html.

LA FERLA, RUTH. "The Star of 'A Fantastic Woman' Picks a Few Come-Hither Dresses." *The New York Times*, 1 Feb. 2018, www.nytimes.com/2018/02/01/style/daniela-vega-fantastic-woman-oscars.html.

LYALL, SARAH, AND JACOB BERNSTEIN. "The Transition of Bruce Jenner: A Shock to Some, Visible to All." *The New York Times*, 6 Feb. 2015, www.nytimes.com/2015/02/07/sports/olympics/the-transition-of-bruce-jenner-a-shock-to-some-visible-to-all.html.

MUSTO, MICHAEL. "Our Lady J Evolves, One Dolly Parton Cover at a Time." *The New York Times*, 10 Dec. 2014, www.nytimes.com/2014/12/11/style/our-lady-j-evolves-one-dolly-parton-cover-at-a-time.html.

NORTH, ANNA. "Janet Mock Tells the Future: Trans People's Stories, and Safety on Twitter." *The New York Times*, 18 Dec. 2014, op-talk.blogs.nytimes.com/2014/12/18/janet-mock-tells-the-future-trans-peoples-stories-and-safety-on-twitter/.

PIEPENBURG, ERIK. "Broadening a Transgender Tale That Has Only Just Begun." *The New York Times*, 19 June 2015, www.nytimes.com/2015/06/21/ movies/broadening-a-transgender-tale-that-has-only-just-begun.html.

RICH, MOTOKO. "Japanese Transgender Politician Is Showing 'I Exist Here'." *The New York Times*, 19 May 2017, www.nytimes.com/2017/05/19/world/ asia/japanese-transgender-politician-is-showing-i-exist-here.html.

ROZEN, LEAH. "For Laverne Cox, Life Is a Blur, and So Is New York." *The New York Times*, 13 Oct. 2013, www.nytimes.com/2016/10/16/fashion/day-out -laverne-cox-rocky-horror-picture-show.html.

SCHNEIER, MATTHEW. "A Model's Life, Chapter 2." *The New York Times*, 5 Sept. 2014, www.nytimes.com/2014/09/07/fashion/will-the-fashion-world -accept-andreja-pejic-as-a-woman-fashion-week.html.

SHATTUCK, KATHRYN. "14 TV Shows That Broke Ground With Gay and Trans- gender Characters." *The New York Times*, 16 Feb. 2017, www.nytimes.com/ 2017/02/16/arts/television/14-tv-shows-that-broke-ground-with-gay-and -transgender-characters.html.

SHATTUCK, KATHRYN. "Hari Nef Adds Another Layer to 'Transparent'." *The New York Times*, 2 Dec. 2015, www.nytimes.com/2015/12/06/arts/ television/hari-nef-adds-another-layer-to-transparent.html.

SLOTNIK, DANIEL E. "Bruce Jenner Says He's Transitioning to a Woman." *The New York Times*, 24 Apr. 2015, www.nytimes.com/2015/04/25/business/ media/bruce-jenner-says-he-identifies-as-a-woman.html.

SOLOSKI, ALEXIS. "Transgender Playwrights: 'We Should Get to Tell Our Own Stories First.' " *The New York Times*, 9 Nov. 2016, www.nytimes.com/2016/ 11/13/theater/transgender-playwrights-we-should-get-to-tell-our-own -stories-first.html.

SPITZNAGEL, ERIK. "Laverne Cox: 'Blending In Was Never an Option.' " *The New York Times*, 29 May 2014, www.nytimes.com/2014/06/01/magazine/ laverne-cox-blending-in-was-never-an-option.html.

STACK, LIAM. "Second Wachowski Sibling Comes Out as Transgender Woman." *The New York Times*, 9 Mar. 2016, www.nytimes.com/2016/03/10/style/ second-wachowski-sibling-comes-out-as-transgender-woman.html.

STANLEY, ALESSANDRA. "Bruce Jenner, Embracing Transgender Identity, Says 'It's Just Who I Am.' " *The New York Times*, 25 Apr. 2015, www.nytimes .com/2015/04/26/arts/television/bruce-jenner-transgender-diane -sawyer.html.

THOMAS, KATIE. "Transgender Man Is on Women's Team." *The New York*

Times, 1 Nov. 2010, www.nytimes.com/2010/11/02/sports/ncaabasketball/ 02gender.html.

UGWU, REGGIE. "Jackie Shane, a Transgender Soul Pioneer, Re-Emerges After Four Decades." *The New York Times*, 15 Oct. 2017, www.nytimes.com/2017/ 10/15/arts/music/jackie-shane-transgender-soul-pioneer.html.

WEBER, BRUCE. "Leslie Feinberg, Writer and Transgender Activist, Dies at 65." *The New York Times*, 24 Nov. 2014, www.nytimes.com/2014/11/25/ nyregion/leslie-feinberg-writer-and-transgender-activist-dies-at-65.html.

WILSON, CINTRA. "The Reluctant Transgender Role Model." *The New York Times*, 6 May 2011, www.nytimes.com/2011/05/08/fashion/08CHAZ.html.

WOLLAN, MARIA. "How to Walk in High Heels." *The New York Times*, 30 Sept. 2016, www.nytimes.com/2016/10/02/magazine/how-to-walk-in-high-heels .html.

Index